T0064285

Flying Penguin

Flying Penguin

How to create miracles in your life using the six dimensions of success

Dr. Asoka Nimal Jinadasa

PARTRIDGE
A Penguin Random House Company

ISBN:	Hardcover	978-1-4828-5294-3
	Softcover	978-1-4828-5293-6
	eBook	978-1-4828-5295-0

Author's email address: asoka@the6dimensions.com

Website: www.the6dimensions.com

Cover design: Arel Holdings
Author photograph: Harshini Thushara

Print information available on the last page.

To order additional copies of this book, contact
Toll Free 800 101 2657 (Singapore)
Toll Free 1 800 81 7340 (Malaysia)
orders.singapore@partridgepublishing.com

www.partridgepublishing.com/singapore

Probably the most comprehensive self-coaching book ever written!

Fly to unimaginable heights in your life

All children can play games on a smartphone, long before they can read. You still have that miraculous power sleeping within you. This trailblazing book explains how you can awaken it. How you can create miracles in your life. How you can excel in everything you do. How you can become younger, healthier and sexier each day. This rare book will show how you can achieve goals beyond your wildest dreams, simply by developing your six dimensions of success: Heart, Mind, Body, Passion, Focus and Health.

Your flying instructor

Looking and acting 25 years younger than his 70 years, Dr. Asoka Jinadasa just won a global corporate award for Consulting and the Asia-Pacific Award for Outstanding Contribution to HR. A UK-qualified Chartered Engineer with a US doctorate in Business Strategy, he is a Master of the Chinese martial art T'ai chi ch'uan, and an award-winner in corporate communication, media advertising, brand marketing and feature filmmaking. Featured in Who's Who in the World in 1982/3 and Who's Who in Western Europe in 1983, he has helped thousands of people reach goals they never even imagined.

Rave reviews

An intoxicating cocktail of modern science and ancient wisdom that can redesign our life

Ursula Kloeters, Award-winning interior designer, San Francisco

Finally, a comprehensive and practical book with a hands-on approach to human capital development

Rohitha Amarapala, President of Institute of Personnel Management, Sri Lanka

If you aspire to achieve greatness and happiness, this is the blueprint; A must read

Hilmy Cader, CEO of MTI Consulting, Bahrain

A comprehensive self-coaching book, explained in simple terms with the thoroughness of research

Dr. Ajantha Dharmasiri, Director of Postgraduate Institute of Management, Sri Lanka

A book for every CEO, every manager and every employee on boosting individual and corporate performance

Felicio Ferraz, Brazilian CEO of a multinational company

Legal Stuff

This purpose of this book is to offer information of a general nature to guide you in your personal quest for emotional, spiritual and/or material wellbeing. It is sold with the explicit understanding that no one associated with the production of this product, including but not limited to the author, publishers and distributors, may be held liable or responsible for any loss or damage caused directly or indirectly to any individual or entity by any use or misuse of any information contained herein.

The information contained herein has been carefully compiled from personal experience, available programs and literature, and extensive research. However, the applicability of this information to any particular individual or situation is not guaranteed. You must not rely on the information contained herein as an alternative to medical, financial or any other kind of advice from an appropriately qualified professional.

The author is not responsible for any errors or omissions, does not claim to be qualified to offer medical or health advice, and does not offer any medical or health services to the readers. Some of the advice and exercises contained in this book may not be suitable for some people. Always check with a qualified physician before undertaking any regime of exercise or change in diet, including the ones contained in this book. If you think you may be suffering from any medical condition, you should not delay seeking medical advice, disregard medical advice, or discontinue medical treatment because of any information contained in this book.

The fact that a person, organisation or website is referred to in this work as a citation and/or a possible source of further information does not mean that the author or publisher endorses the information or recommendations such person, organisation or website may provide.

Dedication

I dedicate this book to every person I have associated with in my life for what I learnt from each of them, and to three special teachers who showed me how to unleash the vast inborn potential I possess as a human:

Gautama Buddha:

who explained the path to perfection in simple terms I could understand and follow;

Master Chu King Hung:

who taught me Chinese breathing meditation (Chi Kung) and the secrets of Yang-style T'ai chi ch'uan;

Master Del Pe:

who taught me Himalayan techniques for invigorating all the energy centres (Chakras) in my body.

Contents

Part Two: Getting Ready to Fly

Part Three: Developing Flying Skills

Part Four: Using Your Flying Skills

Introduction

Can Penguins and Humans Fly?

They both discover their wings
under life-threatening circumstances

Emperor penguins can fly. Just for a few seconds. They shoot up from the water about four or five feet in the air to land on the ice at a higher level, when threatened by a predatory leopard seal lurking under the ice.[1] Humans can fly beyond the limitations of their day-to-day lives, under life-threatening circumstances. We have heard stories of how ordinary people occasionally display extraordinary feats of strength. For example, a mother lifting a very heavy fallen beam to free her child trapped under it.

The seers of Mexico, such as don Juan Matus, explained such happenings as a part of 'non-ordinary reality'. A good example is how any little child can intuitively find and play games on a smartphone long before they learn to read. Why do they lose such abilities when they grow up? As an engineer, I wanted to find a practical framework for doing things that go beyond the 'ordinary reality' of our lives. I was inspired by what Carlos Castaneda had written: *If you enter a state of 'non-ordinary reality', it is only to draw from it what you need to see the miraculous character of ordinary reality.*[2]

While searching for practical ways to unravel the mysteries of 'non-ordinary reality', I found bits and pieces from diverse sources while living and working in Europe, USA and Sri Lanka. Many of the books I read emphasised

---

1 https://www.youtube.com/watch?v=wr4d2FfivA4

2 http://www.cleargreen.com/

the power of positive thought. However, they didn't explain how I could get rid of the negative thoughts lurking in my mind. Motivational programs and speakers were able to energise and empower me. But, most of it was gone within a few days.

In contrast, I observed that every pre-school child was able to learn complex things like walking and talking, without help from anyone. I wanted to find out how they did that. What I found from diverse sources were like the pieces of a colourful but incomplete jigsaw puzzle. Fitting them all together into a complete, concise and actionable model was the challenge I faced when writing this book. My aim was to give 'need to have' information, with a minimum of 'nice to have' background information.

I wanted to develop a simple but complete instruction manual on how anyone can unleash their vast inborn human potential to achieve extraordinary feats, as highly successful people have done. This book contains a blend of concepts and methodologies drawn from diverse sources such as Oriental martial arts, Tibetan rites and Himalayan wisdom, combined with the latest research in neuroscience, genetics, behavioural psychology, nutrition, healthcare etc.

To support the validity of all the concepts I present, I have given a list of references at the end of the book, and links to online content as footnotes at the bottom of each page (mostly as shortened links, made through the kind courtesy of http://tinyurl.com). However, since this information was collected over four decades, I may have failed to acknowledge some sources. My sincere apologies for any such unintended omissions, which I will be happy to put right in subsequent editions.

Congratulate yourself for embarking on this exciting voyage of self-discovery. You can unleash the vast human potential mostly sleeping within you by using the simple but powerful techniques you will discover. You will start achieving goals you never even imagined, as I have done over the past ten years after my sixtieth birthday. This can range from earning millions, living joyfully, getting younger, becoming healthier, achieving world fame, becoming enlightened, or any combination thereof that you desire.

Irrespective of your age, gender, background, education or experience, this book will help you develop all six dimensions of success you have within you. It will help you achieve the loftiest goals you can imagine.

I am the happiest man alive.
I have that in me that can convert poverty into riches, adversity into prosperity, and I am more invulnerable than Achilles. Fortune hath not one place to hit me.
Sir Thomas Browne, Religio Medici[3]

Meet Your Flying Instructor

How often do we find
the blind leading the blind?

I will share with you how I learnt to fly to incredible heights ten years ago, after my sixtieth birthday. Over the past ten years, I have become ten years younger, won many international and national awards, enjoy perfect natural health, and become a thought-leader in a field in which I have no formal qualifications or work experience – human resource development.

I started life as a child growing up in a small tea estate in a little town in Sri Lanka, and continued on a long journey of self-discovery through England, Belgium, USA and back to Sri Lanka. During the first part of that journey, I become a UK-qualified Chartered Engineer in computer technology, obtained a US doctorate in Business Strategy, co-chaired an international computer conference in Geneva in 1979, and was featured in Who's Who in the World in 1982/3 and Who's Who in Western Europe in 1983. I became a fellow member of the UK Institution of Electrical Engineers and the British Computer Society. I achieved all this without trying too hard mainly because I enjoyed working in fields that were totally new to me such as microcomputer technology. I was influenced by an American computer engineer I worked with, who used to say: *The wheel was invented by someone who didn't know it couldn't be done!*

From my schooldays I was deeply interested in filmmaking. Even though I never attended a film school, I decided to make a feature film after returning to Sri Lanka, with funding from friends. My first feature film (*Vimukthi* – Salvation) had its world première at the California Mill Valley Film Festival in

[3] http://penelope.uchicago.edu/relmed/relmed1645.pdf

1995. That was followed by screenings at five international film festivals and an award for outstanding cinematography. I am planning to win an Oscar for my next film that my subconscious mind is busy developing.

My desire to learn new things and reach greater heights in life led me to read many books, follow many courses, and listen to many renowned gurus. I gathered a lot of information, which was easy to understand but difficult to act upon. They all said that I had the power to reach any goal that really interested me, without requiring any formal education or training. I started experimenting with this exciting idea while practising the Chinese martial art T'ai chi ch'uan, Chinese breathing meditation (chi kung) and Himalayan energy techniques, which I learnt from different Masters.

My life really took off ten years ago, after my sixtieth birthday. Despite my lack of knowledge and experience in the banking sector, I won major international and national awards for most of my work as a consultant in corporate and marketing communication at Bank of Ceylon (Sri Lanka's No. 1 bank): annual report development, sustainability reporting, mass media advertising, brand marketing and corporate social responsibility. After my award-winning assignment at Bank of Ceylon ended, despite my lack of financial expertise, I was appointed the chairman of an ailing group of listed financial service companies in Sri Lanka. I believe this happened because I thought it would be fun to head a financial organisation, and vividly created this reality in my heart and mind, and fed it regularly with strong emotion. I somehow managed to guide it to a stable position until there was a change in ownership.

After my tenure as chairman ended, I wanted to share with others the knowledge I had gathered from diverse sources and masters over four decades and refined through my own achievements. I started conducting training programs for unleashing the vast inborn human potential mostly sleeping within all of us, just the way I had done. I used a mix of behavioural psychology, neuro-linguistic programming (NLP) and Chinese martial art and Himalayan energy techniques. To validate my methods for energising and empowering people, I wanted to base them on a strong theoretical foundation.

So I did the necessary research, wrote and published some papers and soon became an internationally recognised thought-leader on human potential development, despite my lack of a formal education or in-depth experience in the HR (human resource) field. I made keynote speeches and presented my new concepts at major international business and HR conferences in Australia, India, Malaysia, Poland and Sri Lanka. I have had my papers published in technical journals in Australia, India, Sri Lanka and USA.

How did I achieve all that without any formal education or training in any of the relevant fields? I believe the answer lies in leading a happy life enriched by my passion for everything I did. As Stephen Stills sang: *If you can't be with the one you love, love the one you're with.*[4] I balanced doing consultancy work with pursuing my passionate interest in movies, theatre, classical and modern music and dance, wining and dining, playing tennis and squash, Buddhism, Tao (Chinese philosophy of change) and Tantra (Indian religion of ecstasy).

I will share with you the simple concepts and techniques I started using after my sixtieth birthday to achieve everything I wanted in my life, including winning the 2015 MTC Global Outstanding Corporate Award for Consulting and the Asia-Pacific Award for Outstanding Contribution to HR. This is in addition to living joyously, looking and acting 25 years younger than my biological age of 70 years, having a razor sharp mind that is more analytical and creative than ever before, and enjoying perfect natural health. My ability to demonstrate the 'unbendable arm' at my age supports many of these claims.[5]

I have validated the effectiveness of all the concepts presented in this book through my energy-based personal empowerment workshop for corporate clients and individuals. These provide simple ways to energise the mind and body, develop mindfulness, unleash passion, sharpen focus, transform negative emotions and limiting beliefs, and stay naturally healthy and stress free. My workshops have helped thousands of people from all walks of life to transform their lives by awakening the vast human potential mostly sleeping within each of them.

I am about to guide you on an exciting journey of self-discovery and self-actualisation. I'll show you how to experience the thrill of freeing your wings and flying way beyond the limitations of your every-day life. You can then take full control of every aspect of your daily life and create your future – anyway you want!

The teacher who is wise does not bid you to enter the house of his wisdom,
but rather leads you to the threshold of your mind.[6]
Kahlil Gibran, 19th century Lebanese-American poet

---

4 http://www.youtube.com/watch?v=HH3ruuml-R4
5 http://tinyurl.com/unbendable-arm
6 http://tinyurl.com/brainbetty-TheProphet

Part One:

Spreading Your Wings

1. Can We Fly?

You have first flown with your mind
to every goal you have ever achieved

I was always fascinated by birds that could fly anywhere they wanted. Flying gives them a higher vantage point from which they can observe the world below, and decide in which direction to fly and where to land. Even though we don't possess wings, we often use our mind to fly above whatever issue we are dealing with. We mentally visualise and evaluate different options, before deciding what to do. We use this ability to fly with our mind in a mundane manner, mostly to resolve issues.

1.1 You fly almost everyday

Imagine that your car is not running smoothly, and you ask your mechanic to see what's making the seemingly-expensive rumblings coming from your engine. After an examination, your mechanic tells that your gearbox is slowly dying and therefore you need to replace it without delay. Your mechanic has solved the problem, and you have to take a decision. So you mentally fly above the problem to see the bigger picture made up of diverse things such as, how much will it cost; do you have enough money or will you need to borrow; how long can you drive before it breaks down; is it worth that risk; how long will the repair take; how will you manage during that time; etc. Based on your decision, your mechanic will solve the problem. After that, your mind will return to its familiar grounded mode, until you face the next issue.

Flying with your mind is all about sharpening and applying this ability to non-problem situations. You use it to critically examine all areas of your everyday life, even though they don't really need fixing. You then decide which areas you want to take to the highest possible level. This is what visionaries and highly successful people do. They go beyond the limitations of their lives and create totally new realities for themselves and those around them. Many people lead lives of quiet desperation, only because they are unaware of the power they possess to reinvent their lives.

1.2 What power do we possess?

All animals seem to know everything about themselves and the world they live in. They know what to eat, how to stay naturally healthy, and how to bring up their young. They know everything they need to survive even under adverse conditions. What's even more amazing is how migrating birds collectively know when to take off and in which direction to fly, without the kind of meetings that humans love to organise for discussing and making collective decisions.

If we're the most intelligent life form on earth, shouldn't we be far ahead of them? In a material sense, we do appear to be far superior. But, I have always felt that we are far from achieving the full potential we possess as humans. I think what we learnt from our elders and teachers was based on their personal experiences, beliefs and prejudices. It fell far short of what we really need to know to unleash our vast inborn potential as humans.

From a scientific perspective, quantum physics (at the subatomic particle level) has proved that the universe is an energy field (even though it appears solid to our senses), and that we have the power to influence it with our thoughts. Buddha summarised it elegantly: *All that we are is the result of what we have thought; it is founded on our thoughts; it is made up of our thoughts.*[7] Einstein proved the relationship between matter and energy with his theory of relativity summarised by the amazingly simple equation: $E = Mc^2$ (where 'E' is energy, 'M' is matter and 'c' is a very large number equal to the speed of light). It shows that matter and energy are interchangeable and that there is a huge reservoir of latent energy associated with matter even in its simplest form.

All religious Masters have taught that the salvation we seek in whatever form is to be found within ourselves. All humans are genetically engineered

---

7 http://www.sacred-texts.com/bud/sbe10/sbe1003.htm

in a similar way. Therefore, every single one of us has the potential to achieve the highest level of success achieved by any human that ever lived, including creating miracles normally associated with enlightened Masters. It is said that all such Masters started their lives as ordinary children, and subsequently achieved perfection through divine intervention or their untiring efforts (depending on the religion). Gautama Buddha has said that the Buddhas are only teachers, and that anyone can reach perfection by following their teachings.

1.3 Rediscovering your power

As little children, we created our lives almost totally on our own using what we learnt about ourselves, the people around us, and the world we lived in. We used our imagination to connect the dots from all our fragmented experiences to build a picture of life. That was long before we could even read. But, our vast inborn intuitive intelligence got gradually submerged as our well-meaning parents, elders and teachers told us to stop dreaming and start learning serious things. Spreading our wings to explore new realities was frowned upon and downright risky. For example, in Richard Bach's wonderful book, Jonathan Livingstone Seagull was banished from his flock for trying to find a higher purpose in life through the glory of flight.[8]

The good news is that we never lose our inborn ability to fly with our mind to any reality we want to create. Thinking back, you will realise that you have first flown with your mind to every challenging goal you have ever achieved. This boundless ability to fly with your mind is driven by your limitless imagination. It enables you to mentally fly far beyond the limitations of everyday realities. It can be easily awakened using the simple techniques you will discover in this book. I will guide you through this process, which I have personally used to reach heights I could hardly imagine even a few years ago. Most importantly, you wouldn't know the privilege of being born human, until you unleash your vast inborn human potential to reach the highest states of human consciousness that spiritual leaders have attained.

---

8 http://tinyurl.com/csermelyblog-tehetsegpont-pdf

1.4 Science discovers huge human potential

Can we fully unleash the vast inborn human potential mostly sleeping within us? According to religious teachings and oriental philosophies, every human can do it. Modern science has finally discovered the validity of this ancient hypothesis. It began when a team of molecular biologists won the 2009 Nobel Prize in Physiology/Medicine for the discovery of a way to activate a 'sleeping gene' (hTERT code) inside our cells. When activated, this code can replace our old, diseased cells with new, healthy cells. However, this hTERT code inside your genes gets 'turned off' while you're still in your mother's womb.

Researchers conducting controlled trials formed a specific protocol to access this dormant hTERT code. Their test groups were able to avoid a wide variety of age-related diseases including many forms of cancer, stroke, vascular dementia, cardiovascular disease, obesity, osteoporosis and diabetes. A Stanford neurobiologist estimates that the hTERT code could extend human 'health span' by postponing or preventing the onset of diseases associated with aging, and help push human lifespan as far as 200 years.[9]

Modern science has finally caught up with the five secret Tibetan rites for rejuvenation and longevity, Himalayan techniques for activating all the energy centres (Chakras) in the body, Buddhist and other oriental religious practices and breathing meditation (described later in this book), all of which help us reach a heightened state of consciousness by unleashing the vast human potential mostly sleeping within every one of us. Modern science has validated the inscription at the Delphi Oracle in ancient Greece: *In you is hidden the treasure of treasures. Know thyself and you will know the Universe and the Gods.*[10]

This book synthesises techniques drawn from ancient wisdom and modern science into a practicable form that anyone of any age can use to unleash the almost limitless power mostly sleeping within all of us.

---

9 http://tinyurl.com/rubynewbee-breakthrough

10 http://tinyurl.com/knowledgereform-DelphiOracle

2. Freeing Your Wings

No instruction manual
accompanies the birth of a child

Whenever you buy a complex piece of equipment, you get an instruction manual. A little book that explains in simple terms how everything works, and what to do when things go wrong. So we don't start washing clothes in a dishwasher. No such instruction manual accompanies the birth of a child – the most complex thing in our known universe. Something that explains in simple terms what life is all about, and how to get the most from life as a human.

2.1 Living by trial and error

Without such an instruction manual, we have no idea who we really are. Neither do our parents, elders and teachers, who try to guide us like the blind leading the blind. As a result, we struggle through life trying to find out who we are, what life is all about, and our role in it. We have to learn everything the hard way by trial and error, since we don't really know what we can and can't achieve in life, what to do and what not to do.

If a lion cub thinks it's a kitten, it would grow up catching mice. Similarly, our self-image (who we think we are) limits or empowers everything we think, do and finally achieve in life. We usually know what we can't do, but we don't really know what we can do because we've never explored the limits of our human potential. While struggling with our day-to-day problems, it's hard to imagine that we can all fly over them to manifest totally new realities, just as highly successful people have done.

2.2 Our role in society moulds us

Our present behaviour is moulded by three key underlying factors:

1. *Compliance,* which involves changing our behaviour at the request of others (parents, elders, teachers, spouses, bosses, etc.).
2. *Conformity,* which involves altering our behaviour to get along with others (friends, social groups, etc.).
3. *Obedience,* which involves altering our behaviour because a figure of authority has ordered us to do so (parents, teachers, bosses, etc.).[11]

As the Beatles sang: *Eleanor Rigby waits at the window, wearing the face that she keeps in a jar by the door. Who is it for?*

Several research studies dating back to the 1960's suggest that what determines your behaviour is not so much the kind of person you are deep inside, as the kind of situation in which you find yourself in.[12] For example, if you grew up in an environment where being different and trying to be too smart was strongly discouraged (e.g. during childhood and schooldays), you would tend to tone down your individuality to comply with unwritten social standards and to conform to group behaviours. We are like clay that takes the shape of a specific mould, although clay has limitless potential to take any shape. Despite such conditioning, you still possess the immense capabilities you instinctively discovered and used during your early childhood.

2.3 Do we possess wings?

Yes. We have almost limitless power mostly sleeping within us. Give a smartphone to a little child from even the poorest family who still hasn't learnt how to read, and see what happens. In just a few minutes, he or she will figure out how it works, find games and start to play. How is this possible? Prof. Sugatha Mitra has found that even the poorest children can learn even

[11] http://tinyurl.com/psychology-Obedience

[12] http://tinyurl.com/psychology-history

complex subjects without a teacher from a road-side computer that is operating in a language they don't initially understand.[13]

This is hardly surprising since pre-school children can learn without any teacher a multitude of complex skills including walking and speaking, by intuitively using the vast human intelligence they possess at birth. Unfortunately, well-meaning parents, elders and teachers diminish this vast learning ability that little children possess, so much so that a young adult wouldn't be able to use a smartphone intuitively.

2.4 Can we really fly?

Yes. I have found seven independent sources that validate my premise that we all have vast inborn human potential, so we can fly far above the everyday limitations in our life and manifest whatever we desire:

1. Buddha has proclaimed that: *All that we are is the result of what we have thought; it is founded on our thoughts.* This means that we can change our lives by changing our thoughts.
2. Hebrews 10:14 in the Bible says that: *For by a single offering He has perfected for all time those who are being sanctified.*[14] This means that the seeds of perfection are found within every person.
3. The inscription at the Delphi Oracle in ancient Greece states that: *In you is hidden the treasure of treasures. Know thyself and you will know the Universe and the Gods.*
4. Subatomic quantum physics has proved that: *The universe is an energy field and that the human mind has the power to influence it.*[15]
5. The theory called Synthesis of the Elements in Stars, that won the 1983 Nobel Prize in Physics, proved that: *All the heavy molecules that make up our bodies were forged in the stars.*[16] This means that we carry the wisdom of the universe at a molecular level within our bodies.

---

13 https://www.youtube.com/watch?v=y3jYVe1RGaU

14 http://tinyurl.com/biblegateway-Hebrews10

15 http://tinyurl.com/collective-evolution

16 http://tinyurl.com/pmf-unizg-hr-burbidge-pdf

6. Gladwell (2008) in his 10,000-hour rule claims that: *The key to achieving the highest level of success in any field is mostly a result of practicing that specific activity for a total of about 10,000 hours.*
7. The father of behavioural psychology claimed that: *If he were given a dozen healthy infants, well-formed, and his own specified world to bring them up in, he will guarantee to take any one at random and train him or her to become any type of specialist he might select.* He meant that any normal child could be trained to perform any task, regardless of genetic background and personality traits (Watson, 1930).

These diverse sources of information suggest that we all possess the wings to fly far above the limitations of our everyday lives. Five-year-old piano prodigy Ryan Wang on the Ellen Show[17] and North Korean kindergarten children playing classical guitar at Chongam Kindergarten[18] both support this premise.

17 https://www.youtube.com/watch?v=tNTlmlQl3o0

18 https://www.youtube.com/watch?v=5nMZdNZvEsI

3. Fear of Flying

The hell we know
is better than a heaven we don't know

Flying implies change. Everyone hates change, except perhaps a baby with a wet diaper. We have an inbuilt resistance to change because change involves dealing with the unknown, which is unpredictable and therefore risky. Change can make us feel worried and anxious, especially if we feel uncertain about the outcome. Learning to ride a motorcycle can be frightening, if we foresee a risk of falling off and hurting ourselves.

3.1 Fear of Change

It's not surprising that we dislike change when we consider how the brain works. We have an internal trigger level in the subconscious mind that is calibrated to send us danger signals when we think of stepping out of our comfort zone. This is a human instinct that served us well during primitive times, when taking unnecessary risks could create life-threatening situations for individuals and their tribes.

The good news is that each time we change an attitude or behaviour successfully, that trigger level in our subconscious mind gets recalibrated to a higher level so we can tolerate greater amounts of change without activating the alarm system. This means that the more you change, the easier it becomes to change.[19] An increased appetite for change is what makes people want to

[19] http://www.suemckee.com/change-scares-me-i-hate-change/

fly high above the limitations of their everyday lives to manifest new realities. Our appetite for such change depends on our mental outlook.

3.2 Being-good mindset vs. Getting-better mindset

Our attitude towards change is governed by the kind of mindset we acquired in our early days, which broadly falls into one of two categories: 'being-good' or 'getting-better'.

A 'being-good' mindset makes us see everything as an opportunity to show how good we are when compared to others, with any failure seen as not being good enough. So we tend to give up easily when things get tough, rather than taking the risk of trying and failing. We mostly have a being-good mindset, since the love of parents and teachers had to be won through being good, especially when compared to others.

With a 'getting-better' mindset, we see everything as a chance to learn and grow, and we see every setback as a learning opportunity. When we cultivate a 'getting-better' mindset, we welcome risk, are more willing to try new things, are less afraid of failure, and are happier by being more willing to clear up personal and relationship issues.[20] We used this mindset to learn how to ride a bicycle in our early days, despite the risk of falling off and looking inferior to others who were able to ride. We wanted the thrill of racing down an empty road on a bicycle, even if it angered over-protective parents who prohibited us from doing so. Learning to fly requires a 'getting-better' mindset to deal with the inevitable setbacks, which provide rare learning opportunities.

3.3 Conflict between risk and reward

What produces our fear of flying is a mental conflict technically called 'cognitive dissonance'. It basically means that you're in two minds at the same time, where one is contradicting the other. It's the mental conflict you experience when you're presented with evidence that shows your beliefs, attitudes and/or behaviours are wrong. Since such a mental conflict causes an uncomfortable feeling of tension, there's a natural tendency to eliminate the conflict by either

[20] http://tinyurl.com/99u-com-videos-Halvorson

disregarding such evidence, or by changing the relevant beliefs, attitudes and/or behaviours to be in line with the evidence.[21]

The first inclination would be to justify existing attitudes and/or behaviours rather than admitting that these were flawed. This is typical of a being-good mindset. Without any investigation, most people would dismiss as untrue any information or experience that points out the inaccuracy or futility of their current beliefs, attitudes and/or behaviours, and then find some way to rationalise their decision.

Your desire to fly to unimaginable heights in your life will be opposed by all the limiting beliefs you have accumulated about your education, knowledge and skills, which will tell you why you can't do it. To eliminate the resulting mental conflict, you need to overcome your fear of the perceived risk of failing and losing even what you currently have by trying to fly to unchartered heights in your life.

21 http://tinyurl.com/crackyouregg-cogdissonance

4. Overcoming Your Fear of Flying

Learning to ride a bicycle is easy
once you stop worrying about falling off

When compared to the familiar safety of continuing with your everyday life, flying to higher levels of achievement appears to carry the risk of making you lose even what you have at present. To overcome this fear of flying, you need to overcome your fear of failing. Therefore, acquiring a getting-better mindset is the first step towards overcoming your fear of flying. This change of mental focus will stop you from comparing yourself with others and trying to perform better than them. It will eliminate your fear of failure since every 'failure' can be interpreted as a 'success' that provides you with an opportunity to improve your abilities and exceed your past achievements.

4.1 Buried fears

Even the most confident and successful people have feelings of anxiety, stress, worry, and self-doubt buried within them. As neuroscientist Mark Waldman has explained, this is a leftover from our prehistoric days when a healthy fear kept us alive. He has identified six types of fear, all of which relate to flying:

- Fear of failure (keeps you from trying)
- Fear of success (sabotages your every effort)
- Fear of looking foolish (keeps you within accepted norms)
- Fear of speaking (keeps you from expressing your new ideas)
- Fear of loneliness (pushes you into unhealthy relationships)
- Fear of poverty (creates a poverty-conscience or workaholism)

The good news is that according to his brain research, 90% of all worries, fears and doubts are nothing more than memories from the past projected onto the future. For example, fear of flying high above family, friends and colleagues can arise not only from a fear of failing but also from a fear of success if you grew up as a child in a culture that preached modesty, humility and the danger in standing out from others.[22]

4.2 Fear is the mind-killer

Frank Herbert's 1965 novel Dune has this wonderful litany against fear: *I must not fear. Fear is the mind-killer. Fear is the little-death that brings total obliteration. I will face my fear. I will permit it to pass over me and through me. And when it has gone past I will turn the inner eye to see its path. Where the fear has gone there will be nothing. Only I will remain.*[23] It explains how to control your fear, instead of letting your fear control you.

As a baby, you had no preconceived fear of anything. Throw a baby up in the air and you would see how much they love the excitement of flying since they have no fear of falling. As you grew older under the influence of your parents, elders and teachers who tried to protect you from danger, your mind acquired a set of limits that were risky to overstep. Your mind still contains this set of out-dated limits (such as not talking to strangers) that were formed to protect you from danger or harm as a child.

4.3 Overcoming fear

When something happens in your life that exceeds your inner safety limits, or you purposely try to overstep them, emotions such as fear get triggered as an inbuilt safety mechanism for initiating a fight, flight or freeze response. For example, many people have a fear of speaking in front of a group. This is an out-dated safety mechanism to protect them from the criticism or ridicule they must have experienced earlier when they had to speak in front of a group. Even the thought of having to speak in front of a group triggers fear in many such people.

---

[22] http://tinyurl.com/linkedin-pulse

[23] http://tinyurl.com/goodreads-com-fear

Preparing your mind for the 'risky' task of flying out of your comfort zone and reaching unimaginable heights in your life would typically trigger a fear of failure and the loss of even what you have at present. How can you overcome this fear? As Bruce Springsteen sang in Dancing in the Dark: *You can't start a fire worrying about your little world falling apart.* There are three simple techniques you can use to overcome fear and worry almost instantly:

1. Changing your point of view to see any situation that triggers fear as a learning opportunity.
2. Using power-poses with deep breathing to boost your confidence.
3. Switching from debilitating NO energy to 'YES' power.

These three techniques are explained in the following sections.

4.4 Change your point of view

This requires a conscious effort to see every challenge as an opportunity for developing the skills you will need for flying above the limitations of everyday life and creating new life paths. For example, if your boss treats you kindly, your partner loves you, and your children are like little angels, you will be stuck in your comfort zone and face a serious risk of stagnation in your life. If, on the other hand, your boss is wicked, your partner is a demon, and your children are little monsters, your life would be filled with opportunities for self-improvement through the acquisition of higher qualities such as calmness, non-judgemental awareness, relaxed concentration and unconditional love. Therefore, adopting a point of view that sees every problem or obstacle as an opportunity will automatically improve your flying skills.

As a simplified interpretation of Buddha's noble eightfold path to enlightenment, changing your point of view is the first step towards a deeper understanding of any situation and developing a higher level of consciousness. Changing your point of view will progressively give rise to positive thoughts, kind words, ethical actions, a righteous livelihood, virtuous effort, mindfulness, and mental focus.[24] These qualities will enable you to fly to any level of material and/or spiritual achievement you desire.

[24] http://www.buddhanet.net/e-learning/8foldpath.htm

However, fear is a strong primitive emotion that is difficult to eliminate, because it is a vital component of a defence mechanism that keeps us safe. Fear in today's life often manifests physically as low energy, drooping shoulders, shallow breathing, etc. Would reversing these bodily expressions (which are under our control) eliminate fear (which is much harder to control)? Yes. We can use body energy to overcome fear by empowering the mind.

4.5 Use your body to empower your mind

Social psychologist Amy Cuddy's research shows how 'power-posing' (adopting a posture of confidence even when we don't feel confident) can immediately increase the testosterone level (the dominance hormone) and decrease the cortisol level (the stress hormone) in the brain, thereby making us feel confident. This means that we can use our bodies to change our minds, use our minds to change our behaviour, and use our behaviour to change the way we respond to fearful or stressful situations.[25]

For example, whenever you feel upset about anything, try standing taller, pulling your shoulders down and breathing deeper. You will immediately feel empowered to deal with the situation in a confident manner. Furthermore, if you feel that negative thoughts are getting out of control, clench your teeth slightly and breathe deeply. This will immediately calm your mind (by taking it into the relaxed alpha state) and enable you to take control of your emotions. Rather than losing your energy and self-confidence when you need them most, this simple technique will instantly energise and empower you.

After changing your point of view by seeing any crisis situation as a learning opportunity, and using your body to empower your mind, you can use the following technique to unleash a vast reservoir of positive energy to deal with even the most challenging setback in a productive manner.

4.6 Switch from 'NO' to 'YES'

The higher you fly the harder you could fall. When trying to continue after a serious setback, your first reaction would be to say NO and throw in the

---

[25] http://tinyurl.com/ted-com-talks-amy-cuddy

towel. This would be the outcome of the mental conflict between the perceived safety of staying within the comfort zone and the risk of trying to break out. This typical NO response also diminishes our mental energy to prevent any temptation to do new things that are perceived as risky.

Try this simple exercise. Say to yourself 'NO' three times and see how you feel. Chances are you will feel a diminished level of mental energy, and your body posture will contract. Now say 'YES' three times loudly and see how you feel. You will immediately feel a higher level of mental and physical energy. This simple technique can instantly replace debilitating 'NO' energy with energising 'YES' power sleeping within you.

There is a supporting technique that can make this energising 'YES' power much stronger, and provide a physical trigger for turning it on instantly. Have you noticed that when a tennis player serves an ace or wins a difficult point, he or she clenches the fist and makes a swift downward punching motion? Connecting such a physical gesture to a strong burst of energising mental 'YES' power acts as a subsequent trigger. This is called an 'anchor' in neuro-linguistic programming, commonly referred to as NLP (Bandler, 2007). Sportspersons use this to instantly pump up their self-motivation by boosting their mental and physical energy.

Now try the earlier exercise with a slight difference. Say loudly to yourself 'YES' while clenching your fist and making a short and sharp downward stab with your clenched fist like when using a hammer. Do this three times and feel the resulting surge of energy. This will make your subconscious mind relate the energising 'YES' power to the sharp downward stab with your clenched fist, and make that physical gesture trigger that 'YES' power almost instantly.

Now, instead of repeating it three times, say quietly to yourself, three... two... one... and then say 'YES' while stabbing down hard with your clenched fist – you will be amazed at the surge of mental and physical energy. You can use this simple technique to give yourself a burst of motivating energy whenever you want, even under the most distressing circumstances.

To overcome any obstacle:
replace negative **'NO'** energy
⇓
with energising **'YES'** power

Changing your point of view and activating your energising 'YES' power can make you perceive even the biggest setback in a positive manner and unleash the physical and mental energy needed to deal with it. For example, when asked to speak in front of a group, remove the associated tension and fear by humorously telling yourself that you will be the worst speaker they have ever heard ('YES') and that your clumsy efforts will keep them entertained far more than any competent speaker ('YES').

This will defuse the fear and stress associated with speaking. This approach works since speaking in front of a group is no different to you speaking to a group of friends, except for the negative mental charge triggered by your fear of failure and ridicule by others. Though it may seem similar, this approach is diametrically opposite to negative thinking, which is accompanied by low energy and feelings of fear.

Part Two:

Getting Ready to Fly

5. Why Fly?

Human life has little meaning
until we discover our wings and start flying

Spiritual leaders inspire us to overcome our fear of falling, discover our wings, and fly far beyond the confines of our ordinary lives. As David McNally showed in his wonderful story, mother eagles push their young off their nests perched on high mountain cliffs to make them fly.[26] We are just like eagles that wouldn't know the privilege of being born a magnificent eagle, until they learn to spread their wings and soar high above the ground.

5.1 See life from a higher vantage point

By using your mind to fly above any problem or opportunity or risk you are facing, you immediately gain a higher vantage point from which you can see and understand the bigger picture. You do this automatically and instinctively whenever a child or a subordinate asks your advice on anything. By consciously cultivating this habit of mentally flying above whatever is happening in your daily life, you will see a broader picture with more options that you normally wouldn't see or explore.

Our ability to fly using our minds can thus enrich and transform our daily lives. You can solve any problem by using a higher-level view, since the same level of thinking that caused a problem can't be used to solve it. Or, you can achieve higher levels of success in any field, simply by flying higher than

---

[26] http://www.flickspire.com/m/LittleeInc/EvenEaglesNeedAPush

others and seeing new realities that they can't see. Visionary leaders are those who have better-developed mental flying skills than their followers.

You can use this ability for material gain and/or spiritual advancement. For example, you can use it to acquire spiritual wealth, material riches, wisdom and fame. You can become happier, healthier and younger as you grow older – as I have done in my life after I turned sixty. Flying with your mind is probably the best way to discover the almost limitless human potential mostly sleeping within you.

5.2 Discover the power hidden within you

An Indian legend states that a long time ago all humans were like gods. But, they so abused their power that Brahma, the creator, decided to take it away and hide it where humans could never find it. It was difficult to find a hiding place, because there was no place in existence that humans would not eventually reach. He finally decided to hide the divinity of humans deep in the centre of their own being, for humans would never think of looking for it there. Astonishingly, as we have seen earlier, this Indian legend is corroborated by the inscription at the Delphi Oracle in ancient Greece, which states: *In you is hidden the treasure of treasures. Know thyself and you will know the Universe and the Gods.*

Flying above the limitations of daily life, while coping with day-to-day problems, offers you a wonderful opportunity to discover the inborn talents hidden within you, especially if you want to reach unprecedented levels of success. Once you discover the ability to fly anywhere with your mind, you can create any new reality using your imagination, and then manifest it physically in your everyday life. As we have seen earlier, quantum physics of subatomic particles has proven that human consciousness can alter our physical world.

6. Priming your Mind for Flying

Your mind has no limits
except what you have implanted and forgotten

Having armed yourself with methods you can use to overcome your fear of flying beyond your comfort zone, you need to adopt new ways of looking at life and responding to the challenges inherent in flying. Once you start flying far above the ordinary realities of your daily life, how do you interpret the big picture you will see and navigate your way ahead? It seems to me that we can see reality only as a reflection of it in our mind. If your mind is full of thoughts, positive or negative, you will not see a clear image, just like the reflections on a lake with ripples on the water. An empty mind is like a mirror that can reflect reality in minute detail (*A painted ship upon a painted ocean* - The Rime of the Ancient Mariner).

6.1 Cultivate mindfulness

Mindfulness really means mind-emptiness. This is the mental state when the mind is totally free from all thoughts – positive and negative. I saw an unforgettable example of the kind of magic that this empty state of mind can produce in the 2008 Big 10 Indoor Track Championships. At the start of the last 200-metre lap in a 600-metre women's race, a runner who didn't have a significant lead over the others suddenly fell flat on her face. Instead of seeing the futility of continuing and giving up, she simply got up, ran like the wind, and won the race by beating all the runners who had moved far ahead of her.[27]

[27] https://www.youtube.com/watch?v=xjejTQdK5OI

Her performance in the last lap must have easily bettered the 200-metre world record. What was even more astonishing was that, winning after such a colossal physical effort, she seemed much less tired than her competitors who were doubled up and gasping for breath. Up to the time she fell, it was not clear if she would win the race. After falling, all thoughts about winning and losing must have left her mind, so her body could unleash the enormous running potential sleeping within it. This provides a wonderful, real-life example of the kind of miracles we can create when the conscious mind is clear of all thoughts – positive and negative.

6.2 Get to know yourself

Our ability to understand, think and learn is generally referred to as our intelligence. Intra-personal intelligence is one of the nine types of human intelligence (Gardner, 2006).[28] It involves an appreciation of you as an individual, and also of the world you live in. It's one of the most important attributes for flying above the ordinary realities of daily life, to reach a higher level of consciousness and achievement. As stated in the inscription at the Delphi Oracle in ancient Greece: *In you is hidden the treasure of treasures. Know thyself and you will know the Universe and the Gods.*

You will be your own guide in your efforts to fly beyond the limitations of your life. Developing intra-personal intelligence thus becomes important since it relates to your personal ability for guiding yourself using your inner feelings, thinking processes, talents and values. It will also help you to make necessary changes to your thoughts, beliefs, and behaviour in relation to other people and the world you live in, as you intuitively did as a child while growing up.

You possessed a very high level of intra-personal intelligence as a baby. In the first few years of your life, you managed to learn a great deal about your abilities and how to interact with the world around you, without the help of a teacher. This is mainly because you didn't start life with any of the negative emotions that gradually undermined your inborn intra-personal intelligence. This gradually happened as you grew older and started to depend on your parents and elders for almost everything. You also acquired a set of negative

[28] http://tinyurl.com/skyview-vansd-org-Intelligence

emotional attributes that became auto-responses to the changes that you were unwilling to accept in your life.

6.3 Managing emotions

Flying requires you to see all the risks and opportunities in your flight path and respond accordingly, without being distracted by negative emotional responses that mostly relate to your past experiences.

Many such negative emotions are founded on fear – fear of failure, shame, ridicule, bankruptcy, loneliness, etc. and finally death. The simplest way to transform your negative emotions into positive ones is by changing your point of view and using energising 'YES' power, as we have seen earlier. Ask yourself, are you willing (not wanting) to face the challenges arising from your worst fears coming true? If you are willing to see those as learning opportunities, then the situation will get defused and you will feel much better.

For example, say you have a recurring fear that you are going to lose your job due to a downsizing of the workforce. Change your perspective and start thinking of all the new things you can do to earn your living, which are more exciting than what you are doing at present, if your worst fears were to materialise. You will immediately feel happier and have more energy to do your job. This may cause you to retain your job while others lose theirs due to their diminished motivation resulting from their negative thoughts and fears.

As the Lebanese-American poet Kahlil Gibran has written: *We are like a sailing ship with our emotions as the sails and our reason as the rudder.*[29] We need both emotions and reason to achieve our goals in life. A key to your success is your ability to transform negative emotions into their positive complements. For example, say you feel angry about something. If you change your point of view and raise your level of awareness of how you feel, it will be difficult to sustain your feeling of anger. Your anger will then change to love, which are like the two polarities of the same strong emotion.

[29] http://www.katsandogz.com/onreason.html

6.4 How to transform your negative emotions

Emotions have opposite polarities such as hate and love, sadness and joy, anxiety and calmness, resentment and gratitude, fear and excitement, disgust and appreciation, lethargy and vigour, etc. Here is a simple process you can use to transform negative emotional attributes to their positive counterparts, just by changing how you perceive what causes them.

In the first column in the table below, write down persistent negative feelings and emotional patterns that you often struggle with. These could typically include depression, sadness, fear, worries, anxiety, anger, irritability, hatred, envy, lack of confidence, frustration, resentment, bitterness, sense of failure, guilt, self-pity, phobias (about spiders, etc.), compulsions (smoking, drinking, recreational drugs, etc.), negative emotional biases (based on religion, ethnicity, gender, etc.), etc.

In the middle column, write down a typical situation that triggers each such negative feeling or emotion. In the last column find the 'gift' underlying that situation when seen from a personal development perspective.[30] This process is like finding a 'weak shot' in your 'game of life', which you need to improve before you can progress to a higher level.

Negative feeling or emotion	**Typical cause of that negative feeling or emotion**	**The 'gift' behind that cause, when seen from a growth perspective**
E.g. Anger, fear, sadness	Unfair criticism of your work by your boss	Determination to uplift your work to an extraordinary level

[30] http://www.outrageousmastery2.com/

6.5 Understanding your beliefs

Unlike fleeting emotions that come and go like clouds under varying weather conditions, our deep-seated beliefs constantly govern all our thoughts, feelings, abilities, attitudes, behaviour and achievements. Our beliefs act like the operating system in our mind. Our emotions are like programs that function under the control of the operating system comprising of our beliefs. That's why two people who see the same film can feel very different emotions, depending on the way they perceive the contents of the film filtered through their beliefs.

Early beliefs that remain buried in our mind will always triumph over conscious beliefs, intentions, commitments, etc. That's because our early beliefs originated from our parents, elders and teachers on whom we totally depended on for survival in our early days. We absorbed their beliefs and ideas long before we were able to evaluate their correctness and relevance. Our beliefs gradually get modified through the influence of siblings, friends, religion, television, etc.

Our beliefs thus determine how we understand and respond to everything in life. They determine what we think and do, how we interact with people, what we eat, what we wear, what we buy, etc. They are the mental filters through which we perceive the world. What we perceive is thus a personalised version of reality filtered through our beliefs. These can be positive or negative.

Beliefs were formed to protect you. Imagine you trying to make an important call on your phone and becoming increasingly upset because the number is constantly engaged or there is no answer. Imagine that the software running your phone detects your increasing level of distress, and blocks you from dialling that number to protect you from further discomfort.

This is very similar to what happens in your mind. It reprogrammes itself to ensure your survival and safety, based on past impressionable experiences and the patterns derived from them. Your mind will continue to act towards you like a protective guide, even after the relevant external circumstances change. The Beatles expressed this metaphorically in their song, A day in the life: *He blew his mind out in a car; he didn't notice that the lights had changed.*

Imagine you were a backbencher at school and had a feeling that other students were better than you. Say you entered university and obtained a degree. After graduation, you went for several job interviews for a position that matched your qualification, but was unsuccessful at each one. Your increasing disappointment, combined with your feeling of inadequacy at school, will prevent you from applying for the level of job you deserve. Your mental conditioning will make you settle for a lower position, where there will be no risk of failure due to your imagined inadequacies being discovered.

An impressive real-life example of the power of belief was shown by Roger Banister in 1954, in something very physical like athletics. There was a strong belief at the time that anyone who runs a mile in four minutes will die of heart failure. He didn't believe it. As a part of his training, he used frequent visualisations to create certainty in his mind and body about achieving that 'impossible' goal, and became the first man to run the 4-minute mile. Surprisingly, his record lasted only six weeks. Many other athletes were able to do the same subsequently, simply because the limiting belief was gone. What was holding them back was not their physical ability, but their mental barrier.

6.6 Identifying limiting beliefs

Limiting beliefs that you acquired about yourself almost unconsciously during your early years might include: 'I'm not a good person', 'I'm ugly', 'I'm stupid', 'Nobody likes me', etc. Here is a simple way to identify such limiting beliefs that act as invisible roadblocks in your life today without your knowledge. Say you have problems of never having enough money, and a string of unsuccessful relationships. Now detach yourself from each issue, and objectively ask yourself what you must believe to create such a situation. After listening to your inner voice, you may come up with insightful answers such as 'money is the root cause of all evil' or 'I am a bad person, so I don't deserve love', as shown in the example below.

A problem area in life	Old belief that created it
Not having enough money	Money is the root cause of all evil
Unsuccessful relationships	I am a bad person; I don't deserve love

Such old beliefs, which are like invisible barriers in your life today, were all based on past beliefs and experiences. Recent studies have shown that we can change such limiting beliefs that govern our mindsets, attitudes and behaviours, by using a simple trick.

6.7 Creating new beliefs

The subconscious mind doesn't know the difference between what is real and what is imagined. You can use this to replace an earlier limiting belief with an empowering alternative. You need to repeatedly and vividly imagine with all applicable senses the desired outcome, as if already achieved. The subconscious mind will then get reprogrammed with this new belief, and start supporting the thoughts and actions that will quickly produce the desired outcome.

You can accelerate this process by mentally experiencing the final outcome, as if already achieved, and feeding it with every applicable emotion. This is like creating a multidimensional filmstrip of the final outcome with colour, sound, feelings, touch, smell, taste, etc. and running it through your mind several times a day. Do this in a casual and relaxed manner – especially just before falling asleep.

In the example given earlier, the two problems that were identified can be resolved by creating new beliefs such as 'I welcome the money flowing into my life from all directions' and 'I am a wonderful person so everybody loves me'. These new beliefs must be brought to life and programmed into the subconscious mind by imagining in minute detail the final outcomes as if already achieved. For example, vividly imagine through all applicable senses the money flowing in from all directions, and mentally experience what you are doing with that money.

A problem area in life	Old belief that created it	New belief to overwrite it
Not having enough money	Money is the root cause of all evil	I welcome the money flowing into my life from all directions
Unsuccessful relationships	I am a bad person; I don't deserve love	I am a wonderful person so everybody loves me

Underlying this concept is the assumption that you are in total control of your life and have the power to change your life anyway you want. This mental principle is found in most religions. The scriptures from most religions say: *Ask with faith and you shall receive.* Buddha has specifically said: *All that we are is the result of what we have thought; it is founded on our thoughts; it is made up of our thoughts.* Quantum physics of subatomic particles has proven that: *The universe is an energy field and the human mind has the power to influence it.* This universal principle is also referred to as the Law of Attraction – you attract into your life whatever you totally believe in, experience through all applicable senses as if already achieved, and support with your untiring efforts. Your thoughts have the power to create positive and negative outcomes in your life, based on your beliefs.

6.8 How to overwrite your limiting beliefs

Old mental programs will continue to govern your present-day attitudes and behaviours, until you become aware of such invisible roadblocks in your life and make a conscious effort to change them. Since you were the one that created these programs in your subconscious mind, you have the power to change them – only you have the password! This means taking personal responsibility for everything in your life without blaming others, as people often tend to do.

Here's how you can overwrite your limiting beliefs with empowering alternatives:

In the first column of the table below, list the major problems you are presently struggling to overcome.

In the second column, find and write the underlying old belief that must be causing that problem.

In the last column write the new belief you will create to overwrite the old one.

Problem area in your life	**Old belief that created it**	**New belief to overwrite it**

Each new belief must be written in positive words such as: 'Money flows into my life', instead of: 'I don't have money problems.' This is because the subconscious mind doesn't understand the negative operator 'not' and will interpret the above sentence as: 'I do have money problems.' Punishing noisy students by making them write 100 lines: 'I will not disturb the class,' can produce the opposite result, because their subconscious mind will interpret it as: 'I will disturb the class!'

While your limiting beliefs get overwritten by the empowering alternatives you have created, you have to start living your new beliefs every day, despite any initial setbacks. You have to mentally create the final outcomes as if already achieved, by clearly imagining the result using all applicable senses in minute detail, such as: seeing the final outcome, hearing people congratulating you, and experiencing the good feelings arising from achieving your goal.

Part Three:

Developing Flying Skills

7. Identifying Flying Skills

You were born with flying skills
that added magic to your childhood

Flying skills are no different to swimming skills. Both activities take place outside our normal life on land. But, flying requires a more comprehensive set of skills comprising of: ability to connect with and influence people, intuitive skills to navigate through unchartered territory, rational skills to select a destination that matches your abilities and desires, passion and focus to reach it successfully despite setbacks, staying naturally healthy and stress-free, and keeping the body in good condition. All these diverse flying skills are summarised in a simple model that I have developed. It has six simple dimensions or aspects that are easy to understand and develop.

7.1 A six-dimensional model of success

I have noticed over the years that to achieve an exceptionally high level of personal success, even against overwhelming odds, you need to possess six essential qualities. These six holistic dimensions of power are symbolised by: Heart, Mind, Body, Passion, Focus, and Health. Though a certain level of success could be achieved by developing some of these dimensions, sustaining success over a long period requires the development of all six dimensions depicted in Figure 1.

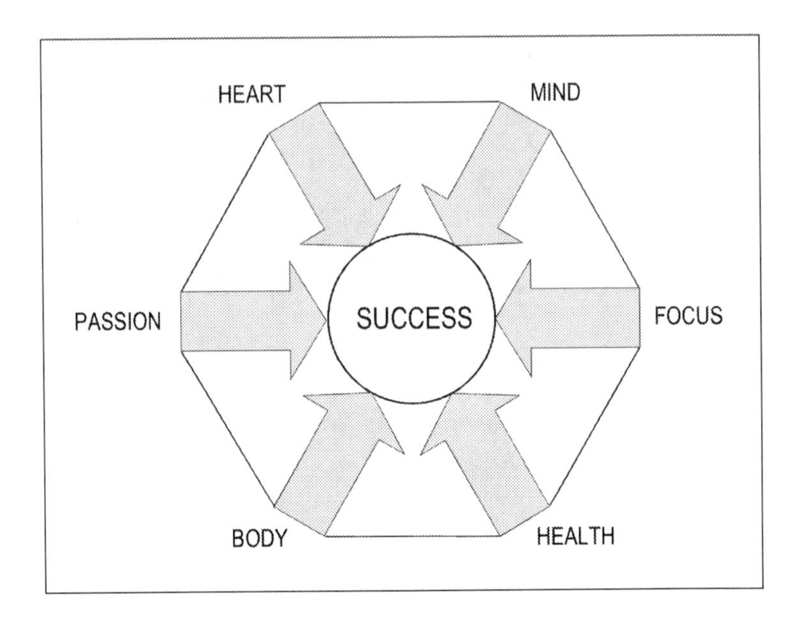

Figure 1. The Six Dimensions of Success©
Source: My conceptualisation

Heart symbolises love and compassion for all life forms, caring for the environment we live in, and the emotional intelligence needed for connecting with others through mutual understanding and caring (Goleman, 1995). Heart also governs organisational success, since a heart-oriented culture will be able to retain staff, clients, and suppliers even during difficult times, and business transactions depend on the empathy between individuals who represent their organisations.

Mind symbolises concrete, abstract and creative intelligence, and our inborn ability to find innovative solutions to any problem of any complexity. It governs both individual and organisational success in today's highly complex and fiercely competitive world. It cultivates critical thinking for identifying and managing risks and opportunities alongside our daily focus on completing our tasks. The importance of developing mindfulness for coping with a complex, fast-changing world is increasingly attracting attention. Articles are beginning to appear in mainstream media about mindfulness (Pickert, 2014).

Passion is the emotional fuel that drives ordinary people to achieve extraordinary results by aligning their hearts, minds, beliefs and efforts. It fuels both individual and organisational success by unleashing the mental and emotional energy needed to reach ambitious goals, even against overwhelming odds. Passion combined with talent can produce strategies that can transform education, business, and communities in the 21st century (Robinson & Aronica, 2009). However, passion without guidance from heart and mind can lead to rigidity, obsessions, and wasted effort.

Focus is the convergence of beliefs, resources, and effort that make individuals and organisations strive until they achieve ambitious goals, despite setbacks. Focus is also about conserving mental energy, without wasting it on mundane matters that are unimportant. I have used focus in preference to willpower, since focus implies desire and willingness, whereas willpower implies doing something emotionally unappealing through force of will.

Body is the temple that we live in. Unlike the other five dimensions that are under our control, we have to live in the body we were born in. Even if you think your body is imperfect, it is worth remembering that all the heavy molecules in it (calcium, magnesium, iron, etc.) were forged in the stars, and that you are literally made of stardust. Furthermore, since your subconscious mind has total control over every cell of your body, you have the power to change the shape of your body to a great extent. If you are really worried that any physical imperfections you may have could hinder your level of success, you will change your mind after watching how Nick Vujicic, despite being born limbless, made a great success of his life using the philosophy: *No arms, no legs, no worries.* https://www.youtube.com/watch?v=Gc4HGQHgeFE

Health is the overarching foundation of the other five dimensions, since it can affect all of them positively or negatively. You can enjoy natural health by using the discovery that every sickness, disease, and ailment can be traced to a mineral deficiency (Pauling, 1986), and by following the advice of Hippocrates, the father of western medicine, who said: *Let food be thy medicine and medicine be thy food.* This requires a change in eating habits to exclude all processed food and beverages, and include maximum Hippocrates diet staples such as raw vegetables, fresh fruits, sprouts, greens, and whole grains (Wigmore, 1983). Returning to unprocessed foods closest to their natural state will supercharge the immune system to protect against disease (Fuhrman, 2011), and eliminate inflammation of artery walls, which is the real cause of heart disease, not cholesterol (Kendrick, 2007). Stress-related and other illnesses can be self-healed using body-energy based, clinically proven techniques such as healing codes or emotional freedom technique (EFT), both of which are explained later.

The six dimensions of success can be personified and understood by using a role model for each one:

1. *Heart:* of Mother Theresa.
2. *Mind:* of Albert Einstein.
3. *Passion:* of Michael Jackson.
4. *Focus:* of Mahatma Gandhi.
5. *Body:* of Fauja Singh (101-year-old marathon runner who ran the 26 mile London marathon in 7 hours 49 minutes, and finished ahead of some other runners).[31]
6. *Health:* of wild animals.

7.2 Relevance to human intelligence

The Heart and Mind dimensions can be related to the attempts at evaluating human competencies over the past decades. In the early part of the 20th century, IQ (intelligence quotient) was considered very important. It was the only measure used for selecting and promoting people in organisations. Later, Goleman (1995) used the research of neuroscientists and psychologists to popularise another quotient: EQ (emotional intelligence quotient). He claimed that when predicting people's success, brainpower measured by IQ tests matter less than the qualities of mind determined by their emotional intelligence. A third wave of scientific research created another quotient: SQ (spiritual intelligence quotient). Modern psychologists define spiritual intelligence as the realisation of the full human potential every human possesses at birth (Covey, 2004). The combination of IQ, EQ, and SQ is referred to as TQ (total intelligence quotient). The heart and mind dimensions relate to and govern the development of TQ.

[31] https://www.youtube.com/watch?v=gCY0Xx92YvQ

The six dimensions of success cover all nine types of intelligence identified by Howard Gardner,[32] and provide a simple foundation for developing each one:

1. *Naturalist Intelligence* (Nature-smart) is our ability to differentiate between living things (plants, animals) as well as our sensitivity to other features of the natural world (environment).
2. *Musical Intelligence* (Music-smart) enables us to recognise, create, reproduce, and reflect on music. There is often a connection between music and the emotions, and mathematical and musical intelligences may share common thinking processes.
3. *Logical-Mathematical Intelligence* (Number-smart) is the ability to calculate, quantify, consider propositions, perceive relationships between things, and carry out mathematical operations.
4. *Existential Intelligence* (Existence-smart) is our ability to understand human existence and our capacity to tackle deep questions about our existence, such as the meaning of life.
5. *Interpersonal Intelligence* (People-smart) is our ability to understand and interact with others using verbal and nonverbal communication, and sensitivity to the moods and temperaments of others.
6. *Bodily-Kinaesthetic Intelligence* (Body-smart) is our capacity to manipulate objects and use physical movements involving a sense of timing and mind-body coordination.
7. *Linguistic Intelligence* (Word-smart) is our ability to think in words and to use language to express and appreciate complex meanings.
8. *Intrapersonal Intelligence* (Self-smart) is our capacity to understand and appreciate ourselves, our thoughts and feelings, and life in general, and to use such knowledge for planning and guiding our life.
9. *Spatial Intelligence* (Picture-smart) is our ability to think in three dimensions using an active imagination, mental imagery, spatial reasoning, image manipulation, and graphic and artistic skills.

---

[32] http://tinyurl.com/niu-edu-Gardner-pdf

8. Developing the Six Dimensions of Success

A simple model you can use
to assess and enhance your flying skills

Paul J. Meyer has said: *Whatever you vividly imagine, ardently desire, sincerely believe, and enthusiastically act upon, must inevitably come to pass.*[33] Everyone has the ability to do that. Therefore, everyone should have the power to achieve any goal by mastering all relevant conditions and situations, instead of being a slave to them. But, despite the time-proven accuracy of that saying (often referred to as the Law of Attraction, but incompletely interpreted), it hasn't worked for most people. That's because each of the simple conditions contained in the above saying has underlying skills which have not been clearly identified.

The six-dimensional model of success fills this need. Developing your Heart and Mind dimensions will help to develop your:

1. *Hard skills:* work-related knowledge, skills, tools and processes for maximising your performance in your area of work or expertise.
2. *Inner soft skills:* intrapersonal intelligence for increasing your self-confidence, personal energy, awareness, intuition, motivation, etc.
3. *Outer soft skills:* interpersonal intelligence for improving your ability to communicate with and influence others.

Developing your supporting dimensions of Passion, Focus, Body and Health will enable you to develop your work-related hard skills, and your attitudinal and behavioural soft skills to the highest possible level.

---

[33] http://www.lmi-inc.com/founder.htm

The six dimensions of success are like six musical instruments forming a sextet. All six are essential for playing a composition. Conversational passages between the six instruments are highlighted by solos by some instruments.

8.1 Developing your 'Heart' dimension

The heart's electromagnetic field is the most powerful and the most extensive one in the human body – about 5,000 times stronger than the electromagnetic field of the brain. The heart's energy field can transmit information between people standing several feet apart. The heart is also involved in the processing and decoding of intuitive information. Research has shown that both the heart and the brain receive and respond to information about a future event before the event actually happens, and that the heart appears to receive this intuitive information before the brain does.[34]

The Heart is more an organ of intelligence than just the body's main pumping station. More than half of the Heart is actually composed of neurons of the very same nature as those that make up the cerebral system.[35] Recent research has identified that, in addition to the four neural centres of our brain, a fifth such centre is located in the heart. Our heart is the major biological apparatus within us and the seat of our greatest intelligence. The evolutionary structure of our brain and its dynamic interactions with our heart are designed by nature to reach beyond our current evolutionary capacities. That means we are designed to transcend our physical and mental limitations (Pearce, 2004), which is what this book is all about.

a. Emotional immune system

Our physical immune system is our body's defence system against illness. We also have a psychological immune system that safeguards us against the long-term emotional residues from distressful experiences. Since we are generally unaware of the operation of our psychological immune system, we tend to

[34] http://crackyouregg.com/heartfelt/#sthash.crsGmbWa.dpuf!

[35] http://wellbodymindheartspirit.com/2012/01/11/the-hearts-energy-field/

overestimate the duration of our negative emotional reactions to life's hard kicks to sensitive zones like our fragile self-image.[36]

For example, losing your livelihood or your ability to work, or the death of a child, or financial ruin would seem to have all the hallmarks of a long-lasting catastrophe. We would expect such bad news to have a permanent negative residual effect on our emotions. We would also assume that the long-term negative emotional bias arising from such a traumatic experience would limit our subsequent ability to achieve goals in life. On the other hand, we would think that uplifting experiences such as winning a lottery or a prestigious award would create a long-lasting upturn in our emotions and our subsequent ability to succeed in life. Our psychological immune system makes both these assumptions incorrect. It stabilises our emotions soon after experiencing uplifting positive or traumatic negative experiences (Gilbert et al., 1998).

This means that people who have had traumatic experiences in their lives are emotionally no worse off than those who haven't. Therefore, since our present emotions have little to do with whatever that happened in our past, we can't blame our problems on an unfair share of painful experiences in our life.

Our Heart dimension is defined here as a comprehensive blend of modern science, and religious teachings associated with love and compassion. Mother Theresa is our role model for the Heart dimension, because she personifies selfless love.

b. How to develop your 'Heart'

Some techniques you can use to develop your Heart dimension are summarised below:

1. *Start with self-love.* You can't give others what you don't have. If you have no love for yourself, you can't give love to others. Just imagine a man, who is seeking a woman who can give him love because he has no love for himself, starting a relationship with a woman, who is seeking a man who can give her love because she has no love for herself. Wouldn't this be like two bankrupt people coming together hoping to borrow from each other? Self-love is all about how you feel about yourself. It has little to do with

[36] http://www.spring.org.uk/2009/11/the-psychological-immune-system.php

how much money you have, what level of success you have achieved in your life, or how many friends you have, etc.

Your relationship with yourself will be mirrored in all your relationships with others. That's why meditation on loving kindness starts with love and compassion towards yourself. After that, you can extend love and compassion to all living beings. Once you develop self-love, whether you are by yourself or surrounded by others, you will be unconditionally happy. Most importantly, you will not be drawn into unfulfilling relationships because you can't be happy by yourself. If you have any difficulty loving yourself unconditionally as the best friend you will ever have, there will be a limiting belief in your subconscious mind about your self-worth, which you can identify and overwrite using the method you used earlier.

2. *Forgive yourself.* You have to forgive yourself before you can forgive others. We often find it hard to forgive ourselves for the wrong things we have done, while we quickly forgive others for similar shortcomings. If you use your newly-acquired 'getting better' mindset to think of all the 'stupid' or 'bad' things you have done in the past, you will see the wisdom and strength you gained through each of them. Learning what not to do is as important as learning what to do! This simple process will make it easy to forgive yourself for anything that makes you feel ashamed, angry, sad or bad. This becomes even easier when you use your energising 'YES' power. When you can have a good laugh at all your past follies, forgiveness quickly follows. Try it now. You will immediately feel lighter and happier.

   Why is forgiveness so important that every religion advocates it? Spiritual teachings are all about reaching higher levels of consciousness. This requires the elimination of all wasteful leakages of your mental energy in unproductive ways. Say you have a difficulty in forgiving yourself for something you have done. As soon as you think of it, it will immediately unleash all your negative emotions associated with it. This requires the keeping of such memories 'warm' so they can be recalled instantly, despite the efforts of your emotional immune system to make you forget them. This imposes a continuous drain on your mental energy – just the way keeping your television on standby mode without switching it off consumes power.

3. *Forgive others.* Each person you have not forgiven for doing 'bad' things to you in the past will continuously drain your mental energy. Here is a

simple way to forgive them and conserve your mental energy. Visualise her or him and let yourself feel fully all the negative emotions associated with that memory. Then, change your point of view to find the 'gift' in the situation underlying that memory, when seen from a personal development perspective. As we have seen before, she or he has helped you to find a 'weak shot' in your 'game of life', which you need to improve before you can progress to a higher level.

If you find this difficult because of the heavy emotional charge associated with that person, try thinking of him or her as an innocent and lovable baby, and the bad childhood experiences that must have deformed its innocence to make him or her hurt you later on in life. If this still doesn't work, using the emotional freedom technique (EFT) described later will enable you to forgive that person and put down the emotional burden you have been carrying around for years.

4. *Feel Gratitude.* Gratitude is one of the best anti-depressants. It changes your point of view and makes you feel grateful for every single thing in your life – good and bad. Feeling grateful is a simple way to fill your heart with love. Whenever you feel a deep sense of gratitude to someone for helping you, or to the universe for a lucky break, you let go of your ego. This lowers your mental resistance to cosmic energy and you will immediately feel a shower of energy. Going through life feeling grateful for every single thing becomes easy once you become non-judgemental by adopting energising 'YES' power.

   To make gratitude a part of your daily life, start feeling thankful towards all who love and care for you. Then it will be easy to extend these feelings of gratitude to everyone and everything around you, including your 'enemies'. Paradoxically, a deep sense of gratitude for every single thing you now have is essential before you can attract any new things you seek. As Nick Vujicic, who was born limbless, says: *When you focus on what you don't have, you lose what you do have.*[37]

5. *Bless others.* Whenever you see someone whose face, manner and posture reflect their struggle to cope with the problems they must be facing, watch them for a few seconds with feelings of love. Then bless them silently with emotion only, without verbalising it in your head. To make this wonderful

[37] https://www.youtube.com/watch?v=Gc4HGQHgeFE

habit an unconscious part of your life, imagine you are an angel of love who doesn't know the local language, entrusted with the divine task of blessing people who need it most.

This is one of the best ways to develop your Heart dimension by instantly connecting even with difficult people by radiating feelings of love and compassion towards them. If you find this hard to do with nasty people, imagine them as innocent babies who underwent traumatic experiences that made them who they are today. When you create a strong positive energy field that radiates out from your heart centre, it will transform nearby people with negative energy fields.

6. *Practise the '100-0' rule.* A loving mother's willingness to sacrifice everything for the wellbeing of her child personifies the '100-0' rule, where you give 100% to others and expect 0% in return. This attitude and behaviour leads to continuing acts of kindness in your daily life, where you help all living things even in a small way at every possible opportunity.

   For example, thank people whom you don't really have to thank (like a cashier at the supermarket), hold the door open to someone whom you don't know, give a hungry dog something to eat, water a plant that is dying without water, etc. Each such random act of kindness, done without expecting anything, will develop your Heart dimension and make you feel really good. Spending time with a friendly dog is a great way to learn about unconditional love that reflects the 100-0 rule.

Your Heart dimension is closely connected to your Mind dimension, which also influences to a great extent how you feel.

8.2 Developing your 'Mind' dimension

Your mind is like software and your brain is like hardware. Your mind, through your thoughts and words, has the power to influence the functioning of your brain, similar to how software controls the hardware in your computer. Your life tomorrow depends on the state of your brain and mind today. Some techniques you can use to develop your vast Mind dimension, as personified by Albert Einstein as our role model, are summarised below.

a. Your brain is a supercomputer

Your brain that houses your mind has awesome power. It is made up of about 100 billion nerve cells called neurons (comparable to the number of trees in the Amazon rainforest) that carry information within the brain and between the brain and other parts of the body. A brain cell is so tiny that about 30,000 of them fit on a pinhead. Each cell is connected to around 10,000 other cells. So the total number of connections in your brain is comparable to the number of leaves in the Amazon rainforest – about 1,000 trillion (one million billions).[38] Every human possesses this awesome bio-computer with signals zooming around at about 268 miles (424 km) per hour.

In addition to our ability to think and analyse, our brain runs all our complex body processes entirely on autopilot with no conscious effort on our part. It controls our body temperature; respiratory system (provides oxygen and removes carbon dioxide); cardiovascular system (circulates blood, oxygen and nutrients); digestive system (processes food and produces energy); musculoskeletal system (enables body movement); nervous system (provides communication and control); immune system (body's defence against illness); reproductive system (for producing babies); etc.

Many aspects of the brain remain plastic due to what is called neuroplasticity. So you can improve your brain function irrespective of your age through positive changes in your emotions, thinking, behaviour and environment. This discovery has replaced the formerly-held position that the brain is a physiologically static organ.[39]

b. How to care for your brain

Research shows that when your brain is not functioning well, you are more likely to have problems in your life. We lose about 85,000 brain cells a day, and we can accelerate or decelerate this aging process. Things that hurt brain function include injuries, drugs, smoking, alcohol, obesity, diabetes, high blood pressure, lack of exercise, environmental toxins, unhealthy diet, and negative thoughts. Things that enhance brain function include physical health,

---

[38] http://tinyurl.com/sciencemuseum-org-uk-WhoAmI

[39] https://en.wikipedia.org/wiki/Neuroplasticity

meditation, gratitude, positive thoughts, positive social connections, new learning, healthy diet, sleep, exercise and a healthy level of anxiety.[40]

Here is a list of simple things you can do every day to take good care of your brain. Within a few weeks, these will produce positive results in almost every area of your life including better decision making:

- Avoid any shocks to your delicate brain through sports such as boxing;
- Avoid drugs, smoking and alcohol (red wine is good for your heart, but not for your brain);
- Control your weight (as your weight goes up, the size and functioning of the brain goes down);
- Physical exercise that provides the brain with its primary energy source of oxygen;
- Mental exercise (chess, crossword puzzles, the game FreeCell on your computer, etc.);
- Simple calculations in your mind, without outsourcing your brainpower to smartphones;
- Pure food and drinks free from chemical additives found in all processed food and bottled drinks;
- Positive thoughts (use the simple technique discussed earlier to transform negative thoughts);
- Positive social connections (you pick up the habits and thoughts of people you associate with);
- New learning (learning creates new connections in your brain, which if unused, get disconnected);
- Enough sleep (at least seven hours to give your brain the daily rest it needs);
- Meditation with an empty mind and relaxed breathing (activates the front part of the brain);
- Mental relaxation (aimlessly looking out through a window with relaxed breathing, etc.);
- Gratitude for every single thing you currently have in your life (as discussed earlier);
- A healthy level of anxiety (to energise and motivate you to do things).

---

[40] https://www.youtube.com/watch?v=MLKj1puoWCg

c. Your brain influences everything you do

Brain usage in our daily lives is dependent on our lifestyle and our conscious and subconscious thoughts, which is a combination of our mental and emotional profiles. Though there is no scientific evidence to support the commonly held belief that we use only 10% of our brain, developing your mind is all about maximising your brain function and consciously deploying its full potential. This is like the difference between your car engine idling and running at full speed.

The American psychologist and author William James has said in 1906: *Compared with what we ought to be, we are only half awake. Our fires are damped, our drafts are checked. We are making use of only a small part of our possible mental and physical resources.*[41] Many people all over the world have transformed themselves from weak, sick, unsuccessful persons into strong, healthy, successful individuals, through positive changes in their lifestyles and thoughts, by using methods such as those presented in this book.

As we age, our brain power tends to slow down and lose processing speed. Without a good way to keep your brain fully functioning, you could become sluggish, lose concentration, and feel confused. Your brain power is not an element that remains at a steady level. It needs frequent work to stay in shape. Otherwise, like a body without exercise, it becomes flabby and weak.[42]

d. How to energise your brain

Just the way computers need electrical energy, your brain needs glucose and oxygen delivered through the blood. If it doesn't get enough fuel, it powers down (just like a computer), making you feel lazy and sleepy. Studies show that by increasing the flow of oxygen to your brain by even 5-10%, you become more alert and your ability to think increases significantly.

Here are four simple ways to oxygenate and energise your brain.

1. Standing up is a simple way to activate blood circulation to the brain. Furthermore, you can energise both your mind and body by lightly interlocking your fingers in front of your chest with palms facing you, turning your palms upward and pushing your hands vertically up

---

[41] http://psychclassics.yorku.ca/James/energies.htm#f1

[42] http://www.brain-guide.org/articles_6.html

above your head while leaning back with your head and taking a deep breath, holding your breath a few seconds, and slowly coming back to the starting position by doing the same movements in reverse order.

2. Walking increases blood circulation and the amount of oxygen and glucose that reaches the brain. Unlike higher-intensity exercises that cause oxygen and nutrients to be delivered to other parts of your body, walking oxygenates your brain more.[43]
3. Drinking a glass of water when you are thirsty could help your brain work 14% faster, according to new research. The water apparently helped by freeing up the parts of the brain that were busy 'telling' the body it was thirsty and managing the consequences. Studies have also shown that children who have a drink of water before school tests fare up to a third better. So when you're struggling to come up with answers, a glass of water could sharpen your mind, especially if you are feeling thirsty.[44]
4. Dr. Manfred Doepp (www.deswitch.com) has developed an amazingly effective 1-minute process that relaxes the mind and heightens mental energy and awareness, as explained below:[45]

Step 1. Massage the eyebrows for 20 seconds.

Cross your forearms in front of your face and place the thumb of each hand under the eyebrow bone and the remaining four fingers in a line above the eyebrows. Your right hand will be touching your left eyebrow and vice versa. Then, during 20 seconds, while moving the four fingers of each hand on top of each eyebrow to the left and right several times, progressively press all the points along the top of each eyebrow. This will stimulate all the acupressure points above each eyebrow.

Step 2. Massage the ears for 20 seconds.

After that, move your two hands from the eyebrows to the two ears, while keeping your forearms crossed. Hold each ear between the thumb and other fingers and massage each ear for 20 seconds by

43 http://tinyurl.com/livestrong-com-oxygen-to-brain

44 http://tinyurl.com/dailymail-co-uk-brain-faster

45 http://tinyurl.com/youtube-com-deswitch-com

pulling vigorously from top to bottom several times. Since the ears have acupressure points connected to all the organs in the body, this simple process provides an internal massage that stimulates the whole body. It especially energises the brain.

Step 3. Massaging upper and lower lips for 10 + 10 seconds

This is done with the arms uncrossed, elbows extended and the palms in front of your face. Extend the little fingers and thumbs of each hand, and loosely bend the other three fingers towards the open palms (similar to the way children simulate a phone by extending their thumb towards the ear and the little finger towards the mouth, with the middle three fingers bent). Place the tip of one little finger on the middle of the upper lip, below the nose. Place the tip of the other little finger at the crease just below the lower lip. By moving the tips of your little fingers without lifting them, massage their points of contact in the upper and lower lips for 10 seconds. Then, exchange the tips of the two little fingers and continue to massage the upper and lower lips as before for 10 more seconds. This simple exercise connects two of the most important energy meridians of the body, which end at the upper and lower lips, thus enabling the flow of energy (Chi). You will feel this immediately as a slight tingling.

This entire exercise takes only one minute, which you could repeat three times a day. Even after doing it once, you will be pleasantly surprised with the resulting feeling of relaxation and wellbeing, and even more important, the heightened sense of mental energy and awareness. I have found that this simple exercise has helped people to get rid of their migraine.

e. How to balance your brain

Our brain has two distinct kinds of consciousness functioning separately but simultaneously within it. The left-brain is loosely associated with the conscious mind, and its functions include right hand control, analytical thinking, language skills, scientific and mathematical skills, etc. The right-brain is loosely associated with the subconscious mind, and its functions include left hand control, holistic thinking, emotional expression, creativity, imagination, artistic and musical awareness, etc., as shown in Figure 2.

Left Brain Functions:
Right-side body control
Analytical thinking
Objectivity
Written language
Spoken language
Logical reasoning
Space-time awareness
Scientific skills
Numerical skills

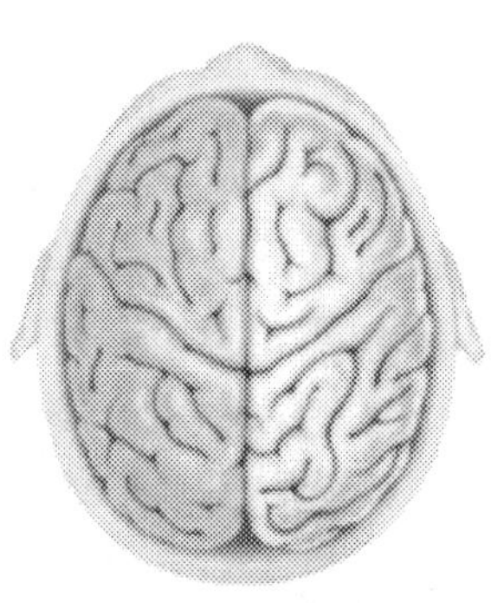

Right Brain Functions:
Left-side body control
Holistic thinking
Subjectivity
Emotional expression
Creativity
Imagination
No space-time limitations
Artistic awareness
Musical awareness

Figure 2. Functions of the left and right halves of the brain
Source: Based on Split Brain Theory by Roger W. Sperry[46]

Children, with their naturally well balanced left- and right-brain consciousness, are like amazing learning machines in their early years. That's because whole brain integration, which means using the left and right sides of the brain together in tandem, vastly improves the effectiveness of our brain. We lost this natural balance as we grew older. That's because our life, both at home and school, got more and more focused on passing competitive exams by developing analytical left-brain consciousness at the expense of creative right-brain consciousness.

Whole brain integration is essential for flying above the limitations of daily life and creating new realities in both your personal and professional lives. It's becoming increasingly important in today's fiercely competitive business world, where creativity and innovation hold the key to organisational success. Here are eight simple techniques you can use at any age to achieve whole brain integration:

1. Juggling.
2. Dancing.
3. Creative writing.
4. Writing and doing things with your non-dominant hand.
5. Playing a musical instrument that requires the two hands to do different things at the same time.

---

[46] http://tinyurl.com/nobelprize-org-split-brain

6. Image Streaming: Creating mental images (right brain) while simultaneously describing them verbally in detail (left brain).[47]
7. Rotating the two hands simultaneously in circles in opposite directions: Bring your two palms together at throat level, well in front of your chest. Rotate the two hands simultaneously in opposite directions (one hand clockwise and the other anticlockwise) along a big vertical circle in front of your chest and perpendicular to it, until the two hands come together again, and continue. If this is difficult, relax your mind and start moving the two hands in slow motion in two half circles until they meet at about waist level, and continue very slowly till they come together at the starting point.
8. 'Super brain yoga': Stand with your feet shoulder width apart. Cross your forearms in front of your face. Using your left hand, squeeze your right earlobe between the thumb and forefinger. Using your right hand, squeeze your left earlobe between the thumb and forefinger. In this starting position, your forearms are crossed and your two hands are squeezing the earlobes on opposite sides. Inhale as you go down by bending your knees while keeping the back straight. Exhale as you come up to the starting position. Do this in a relaxed manner about 15 times. Then drop your hands, relax your mind and body, close your eyes for about 30 seconds and let the energy circulate.[48]

This simple exercise stimulates neuro-pathways in the brain by activating acupressure energy points for the brain that are found on the earlobes. Also, the thumb pads used in this exercise have acupressure energy points for the head, nerves, and pineal and pituitary glands. Researchers say that this simple exercise can increase the brainpower of anyone of any age.

This exercise was widely used in India to 'punish' children who constantly misbehave, though the reason behind its use has been forgotten. Researchers have now found that behavioural problems in children are typically caused by an imbalance in the left and right brain. Electroencephalography (EEG) brain scans taken after doing this exercise for just 15 minutes show that the left and right hemispheres of the brain are synchronised, leading to whole brain integration. This provides a scientific validation of age-old wisdom.

---

[47] http://www.winwenger.com/imstream.htm

[48] https://www.youtube.com/watch?v=42hP6B-VJ38

In recent years, Master Choa Kok Sui has popularised this simple but powerful brain-balancing exercise under the name 'Super brain yoga'.[49] In a TV news program, specialists from different fields (medical doctor, teacher, neurobiologist and occupational therapist) vouch for the amazing results produced by this simple technique in the elderly with Alzheimer's, and children with autism, learning difficulties and behavioural disorders.[50]

Once you help your brain to function properly, developing your mind becomes much easier. Therefore, developing your mind has to go hand in hand with your efforts to help and energise your brain, and balance the analytical left half with the creative right half to achieve whole brain integration. When your brain is functioning properly, you can use your mind to unleash the vast inborn human potential mostly sleeping within you.

f. Unleashing your vast human potential

Every child is born with a very high level of creativity. About 95% of children tested between the ages of two and four show that they are highly creative and imaginative, and have a great capacity for abstract reasoning. Testing the same children at the age of seven has shown that their creativity is much lower. How does this happen? In the period between the early years and age seven, most children are continually discouraged by their parents, elders and teachers from being creative or too smart, and their brain develops the necessary connections to sustain this enforced 'safe' behaviour. The good news is that this inborn creative faculty is never lost and can be awakened by making the brain change such connections.[51]

At birth we have no preconceptions about who we are, what talents we have or don't have, and what we can do or can't do in our life. We learn all that through our accumulated experiences during our childhood and adolescence. Many of us carry various negative beliefs about what we are capable of doing and achieving. As a result, many of us lead lives that are limited by our underlying beliefs, and live far below our vast human potential that is mostly sleeping within us.

---

[49] http://www.pranichealingontario.ca/SUPERBRAIN.pdf

[50] https://www.youtube.com/watch?v=KSwhpF9iJSs

[51] https://www.youtube.com/watch?v=0FWOVJPKjGs

g. Activating your antenna

We humans rarely make conscious use of our 'antenna' that connects us to the universe (also called our super-conscious mind), while animals do so instinctively. Migrating birds unerringly know when to take off and in which direction to fly. During the tsunami that struck Sri Lanka in late 2014, while tens of thousands of people perished, almost none of the animals that lived in the affected areas got killed.

There is mounting evidence to suggest that as more people learn or do something, it becomes easier for others to learn or do that. British biologist Dr. Rupert Sheldrake suggests that there is a field of habitual patterns that links all people, which influences and is influenced by the habits of all people. As more people begin to acquire a habit pattern (knowledge, perception or behaviour) the more easily a newcomer can acquire it.[52]

Different species of animals including humans appear to be 'plugged' into such a dedicated intelligence field called the Morphogenetic Field that is specific to each species. For example, when enough mice in a group learn a maze, all mice everywhere suddenly know the maze – whether they have run it before or not! In practical terms, this field provides the transmission medium for our antenna, through which we are connected to the wisdom of mankind.

h. Using your power of intuition

Rational thinking can only provide incremental improvements, while transformational change based on new paradigms comes from intuitive insights downloaded through our antenna. In over 20 years of research on wealthy people, Napoleon Hill concluded that intuition was one attribute common to all successful people.[53] Chief Executive Officers who performed best in intuition tests tended to be the most successful in running their businesses, despite the commonly held belief that business is unrelated to abstract concepts such as intuition. Under rapidly changing conditions whose outcomes are almost impossible to predict, logical and analytical thinking has to be guided by non-logical, intuitive thinking (Dean & Mihalasky, 1974). The same principle applies to our personal and professional lives in an increasingly turbulent world.

---

52 http://www.co-intelligence.org/P-morphogeneticfields.html

53 http://eventualmillionaire.com/Resources/ThinkandGrowRich.pdf

As General Colin Powell has said: *Don't be buffaloed by experts and elites. Experts often possess more data than judgment.*[54] Founder of General Motors, William C. Durant, was guided solely by some intuitive flashes of brilliance to make astonishingly correct judgments. Sir Richard Branson followed his intuition to launch Virgin Atlantic airline in 1984, despite media criticism and ridicule, the patent office refusing to register the brand name for three years as they felt it was 'too rude', and a survey by Britain's leading marketing magazine claiming that only 10% of the British public would ever fly an airline called Virgin. These examples are in line with the research finding that both the heart and the brain receive and respond to information about a future event before the event actually happens.

On a personal level, while I was searching for a simple new model for success, I did my homework by reading available information. Then, knowing that what I seek will invariably come to me at the right time, I waited patiently without worrying about it. That's how I conceived my innovative six dimensional model and got the idea of using 'flying' as a metaphor to explain its application. I have used the same process earlier to win prestigious awards for my work in areas in which I had no formal education or experience, such as Human Resource Management.

i. Downloading new ideas

As we have seen, we were born with this antenna that connects us to the universe, through which we subconsciously transmit our thoughts and receive insights. That's how we intuitively acquired an incredible amount of knowledge while we were little children. As we grew older and became more rational-minded due to the influence of adults, our intuitive antenna gradually got neglected, until we have forgotten that it even exists. However, you can easily reactivate your antenna and 'download' new ideas simply by emptying your mind and listening to the insights your inner voice whispers to you.

When seeking guidance through your antenna on a new idea you are trying to formulate or on a plan of action you are contemplating, any feeling of anxiety will block this subtle process. If you are crystal clear about what you seek, and are willing to let your antenna get on with it without loading it with doubts and fears, it will always deliver what you seek, perhaps not in the specific form you had

---

[54] http://govleaders.org/powell.htm

in mind. If this doesn't happen, it shows that what your conscious mind wants is being blocked by your subconscious mind in the form of a limiting belief. We have used this concept earlier to identify and transform limiting beliefs we may have. The state of your mind is closely associated with the level of your brainwaves.

j. Understanding your brainwaves

We have different levels of mental activity ranging from deep sleep to very intense engagement, which are characterised by five associated brainwave frequencies:

Delta (slowest): deep sleep.

Theta: light sleep or deep meditation.

Alpha: deep relaxation.

Beta: normal waking consciousness and heightened alertness, logic and critical reasoning.

Gamma (fastest): intense activity and information-processing.[55]

The level of your brainwaves thus influences your state of mind, and vice versa.

As an adult in our normally awake Beta state, the mind is bombarded with numerous stimuli such as thoughts, needs, desires, conflicts, pressures, stresses, etc. Consequently, it is not free to direct more than about 10% of its attention to any one thing. At the slower Alpha state, the mind becomes more relaxed and focused, and becomes far more receptive to learning new things. Children from about seven to fourteen years of age, functioning mainly at the relaxed Alpha state, learn things much faster than adults who are functioning mainly at the Beta level. In the relaxed Alpha state, creativity is increased, memory is improved, and the ability to solve problems is enhanced. It is the gateway to the subconscious mind, and opens up a channel of communication with your antenna through mindfulness.

Mindfulness really means 'mind-emptiness'. Whenever your awareness is totally focused on the present moment (being 'here' and 'now'), your mind frees itself of distracting thoughts from the past or about the future. In this state of enhanced awareness, you see things exactly as they are, not how they were in the past, or how you imagine them to be in the future. This mental state of non-judgemental awareness achieved through relaxed concentration is what meditation techniques help you to attain.

---

55 http://www.finerminds.com/mind-power/brain-waves/

k. How to empty your mind

Flying requires you to be in the relaxed Alpha state, so you have a clear vision of what lies ahead and you can sense which way to go. Here are two simple ways to achieve this relaxed mental state of total awareness in just a few minutes.

Sit comfortably with your back straight in a relaxed position without touching the back of your chair. Focus your attention totally on your incoming and outgoing breath, with no attempt to control your breath or verbalise the experience. If you feel thoughts or emotions drifting into your mind, consciously let them go with each outbreath, until your mind becomes totally empty. Buddhists use this simple practice to understand the ever-changing nature of all things, which leads to a higher level of mindfulness and higher levels of consciousness.[56]

You can do the same thing using a lighted candle in a place with light air currents. Relax your mind progressively with each breath while seeing the flame of the candle dance in the air. If any thoughts enter your mind, imagine how they get burned in the flame and disappear. Watching the flame using relaxed concentration with your attention on your breath will empty your mind of all thoughts and help you reach deeper states of mental relaxation and slowdown your brainwaves.

l. How to de-stress quickly

It is difficult to maintain mental tranquillity in the midst of the stressful situations created by the pressures of modern life. A healthy level of mental stress energises you by increasing the blood flow to help the muscles and limbs meet a specific short-term challenge like climbing a hill. This is like shifting down to a low gear to make it easier for a vehicle to climb a steep road. However, continuous exposure to high levels of stressful feelings and situations interferes with the body's daily functions such as mental alertness, sleep and digestion.[57] This would be comparable to driving fast on a normal road in the same low gear that was used for climbing.

Physical stress arises due to fatigue caused by the vigorous effort needed to perform a strenuous physical task. However, if it is a task you love (like playing a tennis match) there is no associated emotional stress (unless it's a match you

---

56 http://breathmeditation.org/the-buddhist-tradition-of-breath-meditation

57 http://launchmoxie.com/stress-and-breath/

feel you mustn't lose). Underlying emotional stress is the fear of not being able to complete your task within the required timeframe, or up to the required standard. Emotional stress interferes with the ability of your subconscious mind to manage your internal body processes, and also to download new ideas and insights through your antenna.

Many of the conventional techniques suggested for de-stressing are too long or too complicated to fit into a busy daily schedule. Here are some simple methods you can use anytime to de-stress almost instantly:

1. Breathe out your stress with each outbreath. Relax your mind and body while breathing in very deep and letting all your stress leave you with each outbreath. As you breathe out, imagine a vacuum cleaner picking up all traces of stress. Make each breath progressively deeper and slower.
2. Shake the body. To get rid of body tensions caused by physical stress, shake every part of your body vigorously for a minute or two while breathing very deeply.
3. Dance to music while pushing arms upward towards left and right corners. Play some disco music with a strong and steady beat. Keeping your feet shoulder-width apart, shift your body weight to the right foot fully while vigorously pushing your two hands with fingers extended and palms facing up to the upper right corner over your head three or four times (depending on the music). Then shift your body weight to the left foot while pushing your extended arms to the upper left corner over your head three or four times. Repeat this sequence a few minutes to the beat of the music, with your head and body facing forward and the body leaning alternatively to the right and left.
4. Stretch both arms up while leaning back. While seated or standing, interlock your fingers lightly in front of your chest, turn the palms up and push up vertically while taking a deep breath and leaning back with your head while arching your upper body slightly backward from the waist. Hold your breath for a few seconds and repeat your actions in reverse order to return to the starting position. You will feel a difference even after doing this once.
5. Chant the sacred sound 'Om' in a special way. Stand or sit with your back straight and take a deep breath. Release it very gently while saying 'Ohh' in a frequency that is low enough to make your chest resonate. Half way through

the exhalation, start saying 'Mmm' in a frequency that will make your nasal cavity resonate. Even one such cycle can eliminate stress by relaxing and gently activating the energy centres (chakras) in your chest and head.

6. Have a backup plan in case things don't work out. Are you willing (not wanting) to accept the worst-case scenario as a growth opportunity seen through your 'YES' power? If you are, the stress caused by your fear of failure will disappear. This will maximise your chances of successfully completing your task. Making your back-up plan funny will stop your mind from seeing it as an escape route. For example, if you feel nervous about addressing a group, while preparing a killer presentation, idly amuse yourself by thinking how much you will entertain them through your nervousness.
7. Get rid of the 'internal' stress that you take to work every day. Internal stress gradually builds up from doing things you don't really want to do at home or work, due to a fear of upsetting your partner, friends, relatives, colleagues, boss, etc. Whenever needed, learn to say 'no' firmly but caringly. Your 'YES' power will give you the strength to do this, with no fear of consequences.
8. Chew each mouthful at least 32 times with mindfulness. This is one of the best ways to relax your mind. The repeated clenching of your teeth during chewing helps you enter the relaxed alpha-level mental state. You have an opportunity to practise this simple exercise each time you eat something. Mentally counting the times you chew will help you to stay focussed. After a while, this valuable practice will become an unconscious habit that will de-stress you each time you eat something. Furthermore, by minimising the amount you eat and the energy wasted in digesting partly-chewed food, you will have far more energy to carry out any challenging task.

m. How to train your memory

Do you have problems remembering things? There is no such thing as a bad memory – what you have is an untrained memory. Research shows that the storage capacity of our memory is almost unlimited. All our experiences and possibly everything we have ever learned is stored deep within our minds. It is the disorganisation in your mind, not the amount of material, which hinders memory. A disorganized mind is like a filing cabinet into which documents have been thrown at random, with no folders or labels. However, if all the documents are in labelled folders, and the folders are in labelled drawers, finding what you want is very easy because you simply look under the appropriate heading.[58]

Here are some techniques that will help train your memory:

1. Drink enough water. Drinking water when thirsty can improve your brainpower by about 14%.
2. To remember a place or name, close your eyes and imagine the place or name or anything that you associate with that place or name.
3. To remember something, speak your thoughts out loud about when you last used or saw it.
4. To remember something, go back to a time when you clearly remember what you are seeking, and progressively visualise what happened from the time you last remember it.
5. Instead of silently reading a newspaper or book in your mind, read it out loud. This will stimulate different parts of your brain and enhance your memory power.
6. Practise or revise frequently what you want to remember, which will help your brain stay alert and make sure you won't forget it easily.
7. Type or write frequently to exercises your brain by activating the parts that deal with writing, typing and hand-eye coordination.
8. Attaching special meanings to different items of information (such as using memory pegs described below) will help your brain to make the connection and retrieve that information quickly.

n. How to use memory pegs

The memory pegs system improves your memory by creating a simple filing and retrieval system in your mind. You just need to select a list of familiar words that are easy to associate with the numbers they represent. Say you want to create a peg list for remembering 10 items. For example, this could be:

1 Tree (trunk looks like a '1')
2 Switch (on or off)
3 Trident (three prongs)
4 Chair (four legs)

[58] http://www.memory-improvement-tips.com/memory-systems.html

5 Glove (five fingers)
6 Box (six sides)
7 Sea (seven seas)
8 Spider (eight legs)
9 Cat (nine lives)
10 Fingers (ten fingers)

Those words form the 'pegs' of the system. A peg is just a mental hook on which you hang the information. Each hook acts as a reminder to help you mentally retrieve the information related to that sequential position. Because you remember how to count from 1 to 10, associating information with those numbers creates a mental filing and retrieval system for the 10 items of information you want to remember in their correct sequential order.

For example, you can use the above 10 memory pegs to remember 10 items in a shopping list such as:

1 toothpaste,
2 lipstick,
3 butter,
4 cheese,
5 sugar,
6 rice,
7 salt,
8 milk,
9 apples,
10 flour.

You need to connect each item in the above shopping list with its corresponding memory peg, using some forceful action. For example:

1 Rub the toothpaste on the tree trunk.
2 Cover the switch with lipstick.
3 Stick the trident through the packet of butter.
4 Plaster the chair with cheese.
5 Stuff the glove with sugar.
6 Fill the box with rice.

7 Throw the salt into the sea.
8 Bathe the spider in milk.
9 Throw the apples at the cat.
10 Squeeze the flour through your fingers.

Simply relating the item to the corresponding memory peg doesn't work. You need to create some forceful action because for anything to stick in your mind, action is the glue!

The peg list can be as long as you like (1 to 10, 20, 30 etc.). The unique thing (peg) you have associated with each number in the list has to be memorised only once. This peg list can then be used repeatedly, whenever a list of items needs to be memorised. A research study on memory systems has showed that normal people could memorise six different lists of items at the same time using the same memory pegs.[59]

o. How to remember names

The same principle applies to everything we wish to remember. Remembering the names of people we meet is quite difficult for most of us due to our untrained memory. The memory process involved in remembering someone's name is broadly similar to remembering lists of things using memory pegs.

When you meet someone whose name you wish to remember, try to find a mental correlation between his or her name and face, and some person or event you are familiar with. For example, say you were to meet me and find that my name was Asoka. If you have heard of the Indian emperor Ashoka and remember his name, see if you can relate my face to some aspect of the story you know, and create some mental action around that. If you think my face has a majestic quality, you can imagine me dethroning emperor Ashoka and wearing his crown. If you think my face looks far from majestic, you can imagine me as emperor Ashoka's cook, and getting my head chopped off because the emperor was disgusted with my cooking. In either case, you would have created enough mental interest in my name and face to signal to your mind that my name and face are worth remembering.

To develop your Heart and Mind dimensions through the processes described above, you need to use the motivating power of your Passion.

---

[59] http://www.memory-improvement-tips.com/remembering-lists.html

8.3 Developing your 'Passion' dimension

Passion is the emotional fuel that drives ordinary people to achieve extraordinary results by aligning their hearts, minds, beliefs and efforts. It fuels both individual and organisational success by unleashing the mental and emotional energy needed to reach ambitious goals, even against heavy odds. Your talent fuelled by your passion has the power to transform your life. However, if your body energy is low, your level of passion will also be low.

a. How to boost your body energy

Your physical energy governs what you think and feel. Here are some simple techniques to boost your body energy in a matter of minutes.

1. Shake every part of your body vigorously. This is a very simple way to release tension in your body and energise it. Stand with your feet shoulder-width apart and relax your entire body. Breathe deeply as you vigorously shake every part of your body including head, neck, shoulders, arms, wrists, fingers, hips and legs, while bouncing gently on your heels. Do this for about one minute and then relax your mind and body and stand still for about 30 seconds to feel the energy circulating in your body. Doing this to music makes it more enjoyable.
2. Rub your ears vigorously with your palms. While standing or sitting with your back straight, rub your palms together to make them warm. Then use your palms to rub your ears vigorously until they feel warm. Since each ear has reflex points that correspond to every organ in your body, this is equivalent to an energy massage for the entire body including all your organs. Holistic healthcare systems such as acupuncture and acupressure use the reflex points in our ears to clear energy blocks associated with the corresponding body parts. Rubbing your ears is very healing. It creates happy feelings by triggering the release of endorphins. It helps you relax and thereby releases body energy trapped by feelings of stress or anxiety.[60]
3. Do abdominal power breathing. Our normal shallow breath leaves a layer of stagnant air in the lungs, which hinders the absorption of oxygen and the elimination of carbon dioxide. Do this simple test. Take a deep

[60] http://tinyurl.com/integrativehealthcare-org-Ear

breath and exhale through your mouth until you think all the air has left your lungs; now continue the exhalation by pursing your lips and blowing out hard, which will sharply contract your abdomen. You will be surprised to see the amount of stagnant air still left in your lungs after what you thought was a complete exhalation. An incomplete exhalation diminishes your body energy, just the way a faulty exhaust diminishes engine performance in your vehicle.

To do abdominal power breathing, sit comfortably with your back straight and your palms resting on your thighs. Maximise your height by lifting your head while pushing your weight down, without raising your shoulders or chin. Maintain this external form while internally relaxing your body and mind. Start by pushing your belly out as if it were a balloon while inhaling through your nose. Progressively fill your lower and upper chest until your entire upper body is filled to bursting capacity with air, while pulling your shoulders down and keeping your chin firmly tucked in. Hold your breath gently for about five seconds, without blocking it. Exhale gently through your mouth until you feel your lungs are empty, and then, strongly blow out all the remaining stagnant air until your chest and abdomen cave in completely. Hold your breath gently (without blocking it, to let the lungs slowly release carbon dioxide) for about five seconds.

Repeat this process about ten times. Make sure you only guide the breath and let it follow its natural rhythm without forcing it except for the strong blowing out towards the end of each outbreath. This deep abdominal (diaphragmatic) breathing process dramatically improves breathing efficiency because about $2/3^{rd}$ of the oxygen intake is absorbed by the lower $1/3^{rd}$ of your lungs. It will give your body an energy boost by maximising air and oxygen intake and carbon dioxide removal, similar to the way a turbo compressor boosts engine performance.

4. Do body squats with synchronised breathing. This exercise may not be advisable if you have knee problems. It increases the flow of blood and vitality to every part of the body, and slows down the aging process by oxygenating the cells in the body. Stand with your feet shoulder-width apart and pointing slightly inward. Place your palms together with fingers pointing upwards well in front of the centre of your chest. Inhale fully. Exhale fully as you slowly bend your knees and squat down to a comfortable level with your back straight, while stretching your two hands forward and

then sideways along a horizontal circular path until your arms are fully stretched to the left and right side of your body along the line of your shoulders with elbows relaxed. Make sure your hands and elbows move at the same horizontal level, while maintaining your wrists bent and fingers pointing upwards. Inhale fully as you come up to the starting position with palms joined in front of the centre of your chest. Do this in a relaxed manner for about 20-30 times. After finishing, drop your hands, bring your feet closer together, close your eyes, breathe slowly, and relax for about 30 seconds to let the energy circulate through your body (Del Pe, 2006).

You can repeat this gentle exercise even 100 times without getting tired, simply by relaxing your mind and body, and synchronising your breath with the physical movement. Doing this exercise just before you sleep will relax your mind and body while oxygenating your body cells. As a result, you may be able to fall asleep faster, sleep deeper, wakeup with more energy, and manage with less sleep.

5. Chew each mouthful at least 32 times until it becomes liquid before swallowing. As advocated by Horace Fletcher in the late 19th century, this works at two levels to boost your body energy.[61]

   Firstly, most of what we eat (starches, fruits, fats) can't be digested in the stomach and must be digested in the mouth. Even liquids such as milk need to be 'chewed' to help their digestion in the mouth. Walt Whitman (influential American poet) summarised this old wisdom beautifully: *Drink your solids and chew your liquids.* Children with their vast energy tend to eat very little very slowly, until adults gradually coerce them into eating more and eating faster.

   The stomach finds it difficult to digest solid foods resulting from incomplete chewing, especially if we eat too much (which we invariably do, when we don't chew what we eat). Consequently, a lot of body energy gets 'wasted' in the digestive process. That's why we often feel sleepy after a meal. By chewing each mouthful until it becomes liquid, we will eat much less than we normally do. Improved digestion will give you maximum nutrition from a minimum of food, and you will have more energy by minimising the amount diverted for digestion. Also, I know people who have got rid of their gastritis simply by chewing each mouthful until it becomes a liquid.

[61] http://www.mynetdiary.com/chew-more-eat-less-weigh-less-two-studies.html

This is probably the reason why many religious practices favour fasting before a ritual to maximise the spiritual energy available for reaching higher levels of consciousness. Buddhist monks following the Theravada tradition never eat solid foods after midday (Narada, 1987). The scriptures advise them to eat with total awareness, and chew each mouthful until it has become a liquid. Since this gives them maximum energy from the food they eat for breakfast and lunch, they don't feel the need to eat solid food after midday.

b. How to unleash your passion

Once your body energy is at a high level, you have a greater zest for life, and your level of interest in everything you do will increase. You will embrace the thinking behind what Stephen Stills sang: *If you can't be with the one you love, love the one you're with,* which children tend to follow to stay naturally happy. Here are some ways to unleash the passion you had as a child:

1. Do what you love. Start doing the things that used to turn you on, which you probably did when you were younger and less worried about succeeding in life: music, dancing, painting, poetry, sports, hobbies, etc. Doing what you love whenever you can find the time will make you happy, and happiness is the gateway to success (not vice versa!). Doing things that you are not really good at, but love doing, will boost your confidence.
2. Show your passion freely. As we grow older, we think that a display of passion will make us look silly or immature. On the contrary, that's what will keep you young and make you an exciting person to be with. Passionate people have an inner radiance that makes them attractive. In a 1984 concert where Bruce Springsteen sang 'Dancing in the dark', he invited a girl to come on stage simply because her passion made her irresistibly radiant.[62] Moving over to the corporate world, Steve Ballmer started a presentation in 2006 with unbridled passion as the CEO of Microsoft at the time.[63]
3. Associate with passionate people. There is a saying that mentally you become the average of the five people you spend most time with. Therefore,

[62] https://www.youtube.com/watch?v=129kuDCQtHs

[63] https://www.youtube.com/watch?v=wvsboPUjrGc

surround yourself with passionate people who think even bigger than you, and are walking the talk. Such highflyers will give you new ideas and inspire you to achieve the impossible. Find people doing interesting and challenging things they are passionately interested in, and make friends with them.

c. How to manage your passion

Passion without guidance from Heart and Mind dimensions can lead to rigidity, obsessions, and wasted effort. For example, unless you are very talented, your passion for music will not be enough to build a career in that field. However, if your passion makes everything else in life look uninteresting, you may be able to build a career indirectly associated with music, if you can temper your passion with the commercial realities of the music business. Your passion has to be balanced against two factors:

1. We have an 'optimism bias' that makes us think that bad things will happen to us less often than to others, and that conversely, good things will be more likely to happen to us than to others. This bias affects our attitude toward risks, and keeps us going when we really ought to be looking at bailing out of some situations.
2. Our psychological immune system combined with positive thinking can soften the blow of bad experiences and discourage us from objectively evaluating the consequences of a setback or downright disaster.[64]

> *In today's chaotic world, insanity is repeating the same thing not only expecting different results, but even the same results.*
> Felicio Ferraz, Brazilian CEO of a multinational company

Developing the Focus dimension, personified by Mahatma Gandhi as our role model, will help you to channel your passion in the right direction, guided by your Heart and Mind dimensions.

---

[64] http://tinyurl.com/psychologytoday-com-pitfalls

8.4 Developing your 'Focus' dimension

A normal light beam can be blocked with a sheet of paper, while a laser beam of the same power can cut through metal. How is this possible? First, ordinary light is composed of different colours of the rainbow that collectively produce white light, while laser light contains just one colour. Second, all the wavelengths in laser light are in harmony (like a well-timed audience 'wave' at a football game). Third, a light beam from an ordinary source spreads out, while laser light waves all travel in the same direction, exactly parallel to one another. This can produce a very narrow laser beam of intense power that can cut through metal.[65]

Transforming ordinary light to laser light can be compared with our efforts to align all our resources to cut through obstacles to reach challenging goals. Our Focus dimension is all about the convergence of our beliefs, resources, and effort into a laser-like one-pointedness that can achieve ambitious goals, despite distractions and setbacks. Research shows that mindfulness meditation (non-judgemental awareness and observation of sensations, feelings and state of mind, which makes them fade away) helps to screen out distractions and increase focus.[66] Here is an awesome example of individual focus in a complex group exercise during the Rome police anniversary in 1953: https://www.youtube.com/watch?v=fzyGZoFIGvs

a. How to develop your focus

Focus is also about conserving and guiding mental energy, without wasting it on mundane matters that are unimportant. Here are some simple techniques for developing your Focus dimension while making your mind less vulnerable to distractions:

1. Blink more often. Blinking not only lubricates our eyes. New research suggests that the brain enters a momentary state of wakeful rest when we blink, allowing us to focus better afterwards. A blink provides a momentary

---

65 http://spaceplace.nasa.gov/laser/en/

66 http://tinyurl.com/sciencedaily-com-meditation

island of introspective calm in the stormy ocean of visual stimuli that surround our lives.[67]

2. A simple exercise to relax, energise and improve focus: Stand straight and relax your mind through breathing. Place your open left palm on your open right palm at navel level, with both elbows pushed comfortably forward. Keeping fingers and thumb well spread and using a gentle circular motion move your right hand slowly to the right, over the head, and vertically down past the eyes to starting position, while gently and deeply breathing in during the upward circular movement and breathing out during the downward vertical movement. Repeat with the left hand on left side of the body. Each repetition will make you increasingly relaxed, energised and focussed.
3. Hold a visual image in your mind. Place a small object like a coin in the middle of your open palm, and take a mental snapshot of it by observing it with total attention. Close your eyes and see how long you can hold that mental image. When the image begins to fade away, reopen your eyes and retake the mental snapshot again. Repeat this focussing exercise in tranquil as well as disturbing environments.
4. Chewing each mouthful mindfully at least 32 times is one of the best ways to relax your mind and develop focus. The repeated clenching of your teeth during chewing helps you enter the relaxed alpha-level mental state. You have an opportunity to practise this simple exercise each time you eat something. Mentally counting the times you chew will help you to stay focussed. After a while, this valuable practice will become an unconscious habit.
5. Practise the 'unbendable' arm. This simple exercise will show you the power of focus by letting you experience the almost limitless internal power you possess, that far exceeds your limited muscular strength. You will need the help of a friend for this exercise. For a demonstration, visit: http://tinyurl.com/unbendable-arm

   Stand with your feet shoulder-width apart. Open all five fingers of both hands wide, like the claws of a cat when attacking. Touch all five fingertips and the wrists of both hands. Bring them down to the level of your navel. Extend them forward as far forward as comfortably possible while keeping

[67] http://tinyurl.com/smithsonianmag-com-WhyBlink

your elbows as far apart as possible. Without moving one hand and arm, drop the other to your side and relax it. Your outstretched arm should now have the thumb pointing up, four fingers pointing horizontally straight in front, and forearm almost horizontal with the elbow pushed outward.

Now ask your friend to stand by your side facing your outstretched forearm from the outside, keep one open palm underneath your bent wrist, and place the other palm over the biceps of your bent arm. Your friend will now be standing perpendicular to you in a good position to bend your outstretched arm upwards towards your shoulder by pushing up with the open palm under your wrist while pushing down on your biceps with the other hand. Ask your friend to slowly increase the bending pressure on your arm. As soon as you feel it, while sinking your weight down to your feet, pull your shoulders down, and pull yourself up from an imaginary cord connected to the top of your head to increase your height (without lifting your chin). Place your free hand over your navel and push your incoming breath gently towards it. Totally relax your mind and all your muscles, fix your relaxed eyes on any object at eyelevel, and quietly decide 'I will not let my arm be bent'.

As you feel increasing force trying to bend your arm, relax more and simply increase your body height and push your breath towards the hand touching your navel. Make the external form of your body like the outside of a bamboo flute, while you remain totally empty inside your body and mind. The idea is to 'do' nothing. Simply 'get out of the way' to unleash the almost limitless reservoir of body energy you possess, and make it flow through your arm making it totally unbendable – irrespective of the muscular strengths of you and the person trying to bend your arm.

Here's how it works. Your physical body is like a battery with one terminal connected to the ground through your feet, and the other terminal connected to the sky through your head. By sinking your weight and shoulders towards the ground while pulling your head up, you increase the potential difference (voltage) between your two terminals, which increases the bioenergy flowing through your body. Breathing into your navel intensifies and focuses this energy by activating your navel energy centre. By combining this simple energising technique with relaxed concentration of mind and body, you can channel your almost limitless physical energy to make your bent arm truly unbendable.

While developing your Heart, Mind, Passion and Focus dimensions, it is important to understand the importance of developing the Body that physically hosts those dimensions.

8.5 Developing your 'Body' dimension

We are not trying to develop the external physical attributes of your body. Our aim here is to develop the internal energy of your body, which is immense as you have experienced through your 'unbendable arm'. It's independent of your physical strength, which diminishes as you grow older. Your body has several distinctive energy centres, just the way a motor vehicle has different energy systems (engine, transmission, braking, suspension, ventilation, etc.) that collectively govern its overall performance.

a. Your energy centres (chakras)

In his pioneering work in human energy science inspired by Himalayan spiritual masters, Master Del Pe has identified ten main energy centres (Chakras) in the body (Figure 3), which govern all the physical, mental, emotional, and relational attributes and competencies of every person.

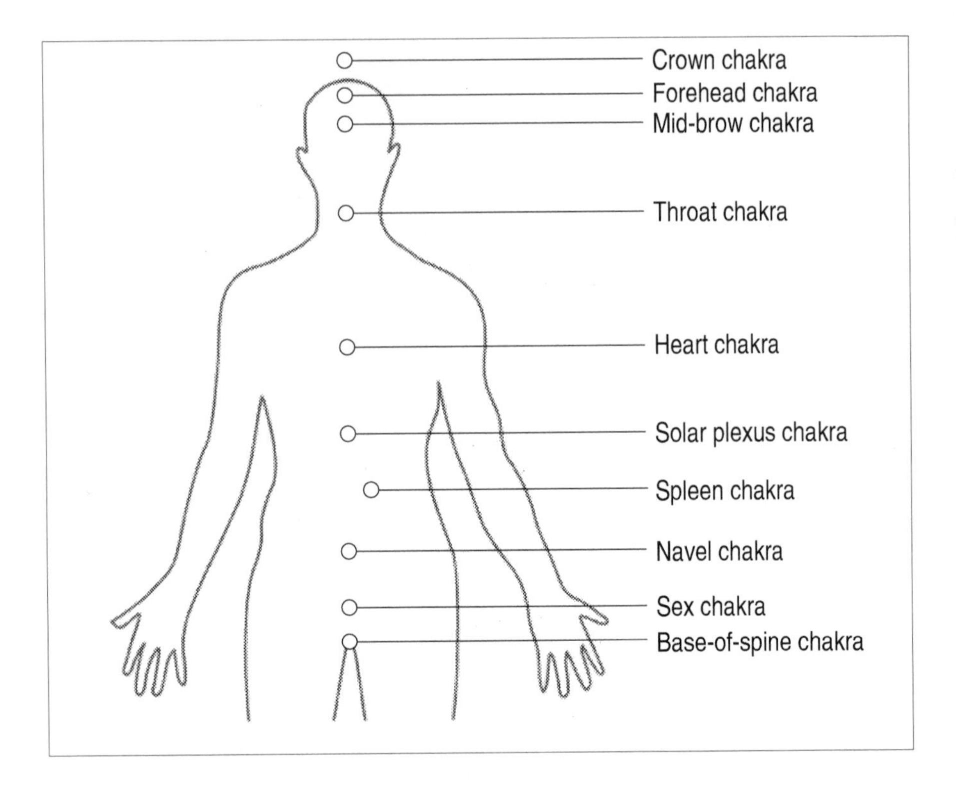

Figure 3. Ten main energy centres (Chakras) in the human body.
Source: Del Pe (2006).

Each energy centre depicted in Figure 3 governs the specific human attributes and competencies as summarised below:

- *Crown*: higher consciousness, spiritual intelligence, intuition, and wisdom;
- *Forehead*: memory, insightfulness, imaginativeness, and greater awareness;
- *Mid-brow*: abstract intelligence, mental willpower and stamina, focus, and constancy;
- *Throat*: concrete intelligence, objectivity, practicality, and producing results from plans;
- *Heart*: emotional intelligence, charisma, love, compassion, joy, and inner peace;
- *Solar Plexus*: passion, desire, courage, happiness, commitment, and determination;

- *Spleen*: vitality, good health, and elimination of toxins;
- *Navel*: vitality, internal power, stamina, courage, instincts, and agility;
- *Sex*: sexual vitality, personal magnetism, creativity, and success;
- *Base-of-Spine*: financial and material success, physical health, and materialising goals.

b. How to develop your energy centres

The level of development of these 10 energy centres governs the level of success of every individual. For example, an otherwise capable person who is unable to transform plans into results could have weak throat and base-of-spine energy centres; a manager with poor interpersonal skills would need to develop the heart centre.

Since evolution has endowed all humans with similar physical and mental attributes, developing the 10 energy centres will unleash all competencies lying mostly dormant within every person. Stimulating the 10 energy centres will help develop all six dimensions of success (see Figure 2). This claim is indirectly corroborated by Malcolm Gladwell in his '10,000-Hour Rule'. He has hypothesized that the key to achieving the highest level of success in any field is, to a large extent, a matter of practicing that specific activity for a total of about 10,000 hours (for example, five hours each day for six years). His hypothesis implies that 10,000 hours of practice will unleash the huge potential lying mostly dormant within people, and enable them to excel in any field of endeavour they are passionately interested in (Gladwell, 2008).

Master Del Pe has formulated eight simple exercises to activate all 10 energy centres. Designed for busy people and requiring only about 10 minutes per day, these simple exercises combine simple physical movements with synchronised breathing to purify, revitalise, and balance the entire human energy system. For a demonstration, visit: https://www.youtube.com/watch?v=AtFAc79Xxxw

These eight exercises are called: Shoulder-spine stress release, Arm swings, Upper body twists, Hip rolls, Internal organ massage, Expanding squats, Body stretch and Side-to-side stretch. The feet are placed shoulder-width apart for all except for the vertical Body stretch where the feet are placed together. Each exercise is repeated 10 times except for Expanding squats repeated 30 times. Since the movements are synchronised with the breath, there exercises need very little physical effort, and therefore can be done even by elderly people (Del Pe, 2006).

c. Chi Kung (Qigong) energy exercises

Chi (pronounced 'chee') is the fundamental energy of the universe. It is the essential energy that sustains life in the human body and can be used for both preventive healthcare and treatment of disease. Life energy circulates throughout the body along channels that are called 'meridians' in the West, which mostly run parallel with the cardiovascular system.[68] Chi energy animates all living matter in the body. Though we are born full of Chi energy, it is mostly blocked within us. That's why people become sick and grow old due to a depletion of this vital energy.

The patterns of energy within the human body underlie traditional Chinese medicine, including acupuncture, herbal medicine and a set of exercises that internally strengthen the body called Chi Kung (energy development). These centuries-old exercises release the flow of natural Chi energy that is sleeping inside us, and raise the body and mind to remarkably high levels of fitness. They remove any energy blocks by focussing on the mind, posture, breathing and movement. You can learn Chi Kung exercises from many sources such as a 10-day series shown in: https://www.youtube.com/watch?v=y07FauHYlmg

Here is a simple exercise I have been doing for many years to develop inner power. It develops your inner power through breathing into your Tan Tien (meaning 'energy centre' and pronounced as 'dantian') that is found about 3cm (1.25in) below your navel and one-third of the way into your body.

Part 1. Stand with your feet about twice shoulder-width apart, toes pointing about 45 degrees inward. Bend your knees slightly while keeping them wide apart, which will make you feel energy surging through your legs as a slight tension. Straighten your spine by lifting your head as if from a string attached to the top of your skull, while tucking your chin in close to your chest, and rocking your pelvis forward. Check your reflection in a side mirror to make sure your entire spine is straight.

Bring each hand in front of your chest, spread the thumbs wide while keeping the other four fingers straight and together. Bring your two hands together to make the tips of your thumbs and forefingers and middle fingers touch lightly. Your two palms should be open and on the same vertical plane. In this position, the space between the tips of your thumbs and forefingers that are touching will look like a long inverted leaf with the stem pointing

[68] http://tinyurl.com/qigonginstitute-meridians-pdf

downward. While maintaining this position of the two palms at the level of your chest, push them forward as far as comfortably possible while keeping your elbows wide apart (imagine touching a wall in front of you with the open palms and all fingers of both hands). Your extended arms will now be horizontal and slightly below the level of your shoulders, and your will feel energy flowing through them as a slight tension.

Hold this position while letting go of all stiffness or tension in your body. Your body should become like a flute (hard outside shell with hollow inside) to enable your Chi to circulate freely. Count slowly from one upwards feeling your mind and body relaxing more and more with each count. Breathe calmly and deeply into your Tan Tien with your entire attention focussed on the breath. With each outgoing breath, let go of all physical tension and thoughts until your body and mind feel completely empty. Any discomfort you feel will melt away as you relax the affected body part with each breath. Continue as long as you feel comfortable to do so.

Part 2. While maintaining the same body and arm positions, without losing contact between the two thumbs, forefingers and middle fingers, rotate the two hands from the wrists forward and downward until your palms face you with your outstretched fingers pointing downward, Then swing the two arms from the shoulder down until the stretched tips of your fingers touch a point just below your navel. Then slowly bring your two wrists closer to your body while slipping the outstretched fingers of you right hand underneath those of your left hand, while maintaining contact between the tips of your outstretched thumbs. Your objective should be to create a large circle around your navel with the outstretched fingers and thumbs of your two hands, while pushing your elbows in front of your body. Your two hands will form the two halves of this large circle, with the four fingers of your left hand placed over the four fingers of your right hand. Breathe as before and count until you reach the same number as before.

Finish by slowing returning to your normal standing position, and shaking your arms and each leg a few times to relax them. Figure 4 shows the body positions of Parts 1 and 2 of this exercise.

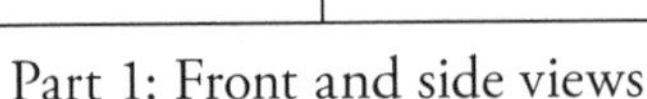

Part 1: Front and side views

Part 2: Front and side views

Figure 4. Exercise to develop inner power energy

Propelled by natural strength,
you are as strong as a dragon.
Inhaling and exhaling naturally and quietly,
you perceive the mechanism of all movement.
In motion you are like the angry tiger,
in quietness you are like the hibernating dragon.
Master Wang Xiang Thai[69]

d. Five Tibetan exercises for rejuvenation

A book written by Peter Kelder in 1985 entitled 'The ancient secret of the fountain of youth' described for the first time an exercise program used by Tibetan monks to stay young and live unbelievably long, vibrant and healthy lives. These centuries-old 'Tibetan Rites' of rejuvenation are believed to have been brought to USA by a British Naval officer in the 1930's. They are thought to restore the normal spin of the energy centres (chakras) of the body, which helps to restore vibrant health. The Tibetans claim that these exercises activate and stimulate the seven key chakras that in turn stimulate all the glands of the endocrine system, which regulates the body's overall functioning and aging process.[70]

69 http://www.eso-garden.com/specials/the_way_of_energy.pdf

70 http://www.valter.saask.ee/files/Five_Tibetan.pdf

The Tibetan Rites are a series of five simple exercises that can be learnt in a few minutes and take about 10-15 minutes to complete. They can be done anywhere where there's enough space to lie down. The exercises combine deep breathing with slow movements. The first exercise only involves turning around in a circle. In the second exercise you lie down on your back and raise your legs vertically in the air while keeping your chin on your chest. The third exercise is a back-stretching exercise done while kneeling. The fourth one is making a 'bridge' with the body with palms and feet on the ground. The fifth one is a bending exercise that arches the body upward and downward with hands and feet resting on the ground.

Each exercise is done 21 times, preferably at the same time each day on an empty stomach. You can begin with 1-5 repetitions of each exercise and gradually increase up to 21 times. For a full demonstration of each of the five Rites, visit: https://www.youtube.com/watch?v=2qLKhvsfQKc

Judging from the amazing results shown by Tibetan monks, this ancient rite could be a way to activate the 'sleeping gene' (hTERT code) inside our cells, which when activated can replace old, diseased cells with new, healthy cells and prolong life.

8.6 Developing your 'Health' dimension

Most studies have focussed on disease, while very few have studied health. This section provides a result-oriented approach to health, based on information gathered from diverse sources. It is not intended as a substitute for consulting with your physician, but raises issues that you may wish to consider since you are dealing with your own health. It summarises what I have been practising for many years to enjoy perfect health and to look, feel and act at least 25 years younger than 70 years, without the help of any medicine produced by the pharmaceutical industry. This section is all about understanding the factors that affect your health, and taking personal responsibility for getting and staying healthy, rather than thoughtlessly delegating it to medical practitioners – concepts that are very much in line with the mindset of a highflyer.

a. Are we becoming healthier or sicker?

Ask yourself the following questions: When compared to your childhood days, are there more doctors or fewer doctors? Are they richer or poorer? Are there more pharmacies or fewer pharmacies? Are there more hospitals or fewer hospitals? Are people sicker or healthier? Your answers will show you whether the medical and pharmaceutical industries are delivering less value or more value to the people. If you think that there could be a problem, the key question would be: What can I do to take charge of my own health? You will find many answers in this section.

As a child growing up in a little town called Deniyaya in Sri Lanka 70 years ago, I can't remember ever going to see a doctor (there was only one medical officer for the entire town) or a dentist, or going to the hospital (there was only one for the entire area, where people went mostly for surgery or complicated childbirth). People seemed very healthy and led very active lives right through to old age. The children I went to school with were rarely ill. The little illnesses we had were cured very quickly by our age-old herbal medicine. This is very different to the situation today, where children attending affluent schools in Colombo fall frequently ill and end up in hospital.

What has changed over the past 70-odd years? First of all, there were no school buses or vans, so we all walked several kilometres every day to and from school (oxygenated our body cells). It rained very often, so getting wet and coming home with shoes filled with water was a common occurrence (boosted our immune system). To buy things we had to go to town that was far away, so almost everything we ate (except rice, lentils, dried fish and spices) was home-grown and included many garden-fresh greens (with oxygenating chlorophyll). There were no supermarkets, and we never ate anything from a packet or can, and never drank anything from a bottle (unprocessed natural food & beverages, with no chemical additives).

b. Primitive vs. modern diets

Years ago, Dr. Weston A. Price made a comprehensive study of peoples untouched by modern civilisation in the then isolated parts of Swiss Alps, northern Italy, Isle of Man, New Hebrides, Australia, New Zealand, Africa, South American jungles, Alaska, north of Canada, and South Pacific islands. Though their diets were often very limited and 'unbalanced', he found that their bodies stayed free from disease, with no incidence of cancer, ulcers, high blood pressure, tuberculosis, heart and kidney diseases, multiple sclerosis, and cerebral palsy.[71] Sir Robert McCarrison, who investigated the health of the

---

[71] http://www.naturalhealingtools.com/articles/weston_a_price.pdf

Hunzas living high in the Himalayas, also found the same.[72] Though their foods were limited, they had great endurance. As mountain guides, they could carry back-breaking loads over precipitous cliffs, laughing and singing.

At about the same time, a group of Mormon medical missionaries, who examined more than a million natives in central Africa, also found no disease, no cancer, no crime, no insanity, no alcoholics and no drug addicts among them. A similar group also found no such disorders among primitive peoples in South America. When the same investigators studied diseases in villages only a few miles away, where white people had brought products of civilisation such as white sugar and white flour, they found ulcers, heart and kidney diseases, cancer, high blood pressure, colitis and tuberculosis. In Africa and South America, the medical missionaries found cancer rampant among members of the same tribes, who had earlier stayed cancer free on their native diets (Davies, 1970). Dr. Price's comprehensive study found tuberculosis, tooth decay and deformed dental arches, faces and feet in tribes living in many different parts of the world, with many such problems appearing in children of the first generation after adoption of modern foods by their parents.

c. Problem with the medical industry

We trust the ability of doctors to diagnose our illnesses accurately and prescribe the correct drugs. However, doctors treating patients apply an ad hoc, trial-and-error approach. They say that if one drug doesn't work, not to worry, they will give you another one. Even worse, if you consult two different doctors regarding the same serious ailment, chances are they will give you two different medications, and even disagree with the medicines prescribed by the other one. This means that we are the guinea pigs paying for their experiments. We have to start taking more interest in our own health, since doctors don't seem to have the time or the inclination to study new developments in their fields.

For example, many doctors are prescribing statin drugs and recommending a low-fat diet to lower cholesterol levels, despite the discovery that the real cause of heart disease is not elevated blood cholesterol, but chronic inflammation in the artery wall. Main causes of such inflammation are the overload of simple, highly processed carbohydrates (sugar, flour and all the products made from them) and the excessive consumption of omega-6 vegetable oils like soybean,

---

72 http://www.byregion.net/articles-healers/Hunza_Diet.html

corn and sunflower that are also found in many processed foods. Mainstream medicine made a terrible mistake when it advised people to avoid saturated fat in favour of foods high in omega-6 fats. Animal fats such as butter contain less than 20% omega-6 and are much less likely to cause inflammation than the supposedly healthy oils labelled polyunsaturated.[73]

Research also shows that statins are mostly ineffective and have many more side effects than has been admitted. As the most profitable drug in the history of medicine, in order to convince millions of people to spend billions on statins, the pharmaceutical industry is claiming that statins are wonder-drugs that offer unparalleled protection against heart disease. The unquestioning medical profession is continuing to prescribe statins, ignoring all the studies and reports that suggest they shouldn't.[74]

In an evidence-based estimate of patient harms associated with hospital care in the US in 2013, the number of premature deaths associated with preventable harm to patients was estimated at more than 400,000 per year. Serious harm seemed to be 10 to 20 times more common than lethal harm (4 to 8 million patients seriously harmed).[75] According to a WHO update in June 2014, an estimated one in 10 patients is harmed while receiving hospital care in developed countries.[76]

d. Problem with modern drugs

Modern drugs (such as penicillin, called the most important medical innovation of the 20th century) have saved millions of lives. However, every drug, without exception, is toxic to some extent. They induce stress and produce dietary deficiencies by destroying nutrients, using them up, preventing their absorption, increasing their excretion, or chemically taking their place. Since drugs are taken during illness, their toxicity occurs at a time when a person is least able to cope with it. Also, drugs released for human use are tested on healthy animals suffering from no deficiencies, and then given to ill persons who are suffering from many (Davis, 1972). The key question is: Is the ability of drugs to cure illnesses greater than the risk posed by their toxicity?

---

73 http://tinyurl.com/sott-net-HeartSurgeon

74 http://tinyurl.com/westonapricefoundation

75 http://www.ncbi.nlm.nih.gov/pubmed/23860193

76 http://www.who.int/features/factfiles/patient_safety/en/

A fully-referenced research report in the early 2000's, 'Death by Medicine', presented compelling evidence to show that the American medical system was the leading cause of death and injury in the US: 2.2 million people per year having adverse reactions to prescribed drugs in hospitals; 20 million unnecessary antibiotics prescribed annually for viral infections; 7.5 million unnecessary medical and surgical procedures performed annually; 8.9 million people exposed to unnecessary hospitalisation per year. The total number of deaths caused by legal drugs prescribed by a medical doctor in 2001 was 783,936 whereas the number attributable to heart disease was 699,697 and the number attributable to cancer was 553,251. The estimated 10-year total of 7.8 million iatrogenic deaths (medical or doctor induced) is more than all the casualties from all the wars fought by the US in its entire history.[77]

This research report also states that, according to an ABC news report at that time, pharmaceutical companies spent over US$ 2 billion a year on over 314,000 events attended by doctors; a survey of clinical trials revealed that when a drug company funds a study, there is a 90% chance that the drug will be perceived as effective, whereas a non-drug-company-funded study will show favourable results only 50% of the time, suggesting that though money can't buy love, it can buy any 'scientific' result desired. In 1981, the drug industry 'gave' US$ 292 million to colleges and universities for research; by 1991, this figure had risen to US$ 2.1 billion.

---

77 http://www.webdc.com/pdfs/deathbymedicine.pdf

Dr. Allen Roses, worldwide vice-president of genetics at GlaxoSmithKline (GSK), has admitted that most prescription medicines do not work on most people who take them. He has said that the vast majority of drugs (more than 90%) only work in 30 to 50% of the people, and that less than half of the patients prescribed some of the most expensive drugs actually derived any benefit from them. Drugs for Alzheimer's disease work in less than one in three patients; drugs for cancer are only effective in a quarter of patients; drugs for migraines, osteoporosis, and arthritis work in about half the patients. His admission goes against a marketing culture within the industry that has relied on selling as many drugs as possible to the widest number of patients – a culture that has made GSK one of the most profitable pharmaceuticals companies, but which has also meant that most of its drugs are at best useless, and even possibly dangerous, for many patients.[78]

e. Pharmaceutical industry's dilemma

Every industry tries to produce better products that deliver higher value at a lower price, as a vehicle for their growth. Unfortunately, the pharmaceutical industry can't afford to do that. If they produce medicines that heal illnesses, their revenues will come down drastically. So instead of finding cures or preventions, they develop drugs to profitably 'manage' the symptoms of disease through life-long medication. It's not in their financial interest to find real cures that would cut off their profits. That's why they actively block the science and research for natural cures. That's why they spend an estimated US$ 180 million annually in the US on lobbyists to push through legislation on their behalf, and leverage their control over the US Food and Drugs Administration (FDA) to guarantee no disease-curing drug gets to market.[79]

For example, a specific kind of tree produces the strongest natural anti-cancer molecules in existence called acetogenins. First isolated by Dr. Jerry McLaughlin from Purdue University, they have been through over 341 scientific studies. Many such research reports were peer-reviewed and published in respected journals like The Journal of Medicinal Chemistry, Life Sciences Journal, Cancer Letters, etc. They all lead to one incredible conclusion: Acetogenins can stop cancer cells dead in their tracks and reverse tumour

---

[78] http://tinyurl.com/independent-co-uk-GlaxoChief

[79] http://tinyurl.com/rubynewbee-breakthrough

growth. One study even reported an acetogenin that's up to 250 times more potent than Adriamycin (a leading chemotherapy drug), with zero serious side effects. Patients using acetogenin therapy suffered no damage whatsoever to healthy cells, which is totally unheard of. Dr. McLaughlin has said: *People that were given only a couple months to live are surpassing their doctors' expectations in a marvellous way. Those that were weakened or bed-ridden have more energy to do the things they enjoy... And even more promising are the reductions in tumour size without hair loss, nausea, or other side effects.*[80]

Why are ground-breaking findings like these from distinguished scientists, published in major scientific journals, not hitting media headlines and getting widely adopted? The first company to extract acetogenins and make them available to the public, called Raintree Nutrition that specialised in rainforest plants, has been forced to shut down. Leslie Taylor, who founded the company, has explained why: *Regulations enforced by the FDA have progressively prohibited free speech about the benefits of herbal supplements – what to take them for and how to use them.*[81]

With over US$ 132 billion expended each year for diabetes care in the United States alone, the manufacturers of drugs and diabetes products make serious money off the disease. Diabetes has now reached epidemic proportions and is a lifelong disease. This makes it, the 'perfect disease' for the pharmaceutical industry.[82] Do they have any incentive to find a cure for it?

f. Healing illnesses without drugs

Is diabetes a chronic disease that has no cure, as claimed by the American Diabetes Association? 'Simply Raw: Reversing diabetes in 30 days' is an independent documentary film that chronicles six Americans with diabetes who switch to a diet consisting entirely of vegan, organic, uncooked food in order to reverse diabetes without pharmaceutical medication. After 30 days, their blood sugar has stabilised and they had effectively reversed their diabetes.[83]

How is that possible? We have become so drug-addicted that the idea of healing illnesses just through diet sounds ridiculous. However, Hippocrates,

---

80 http://tinyurl.com/HealthSciencesInstitute
81 http://www.rain-tree.com/rtmprod.htm#.VdAQ0vmqqko
82 http://tinyurl.com/diabeteshealth-com-Profitable
83 http://tinyurl.com/topdocumentaryfilms-diabetes

the father of Western medicine has said: *Let food be your medicine and medicine your food.*[84] The Hippocrates diet allows the body to correct its problems naturally and at its own pace. Through a diet of fresh fruits, vegetables, grains, nuts, and super nutritious foods such as sprouts and wheatgrass juice, all of which are prepared without cooking, the body is able to restore its internal balance and maintain a healthy weight, fight disease, and heal itself (Wigmore, 1983). Your immune system holds the key to natural health without medicines.

g. Strengthening your immune system

The immune system is a network of cells, tissues, and organs that work together to defend the body against attacks by external invaders. These are primarily microbes (germs) that are tiny, infection-causing organisms such as bacteria, viruses, parasites, and fungi. Because the human body provides an ideal environment for many microbes, they try to break in. It is the immune system's job to keep them out, or failing that, to seek out and destroy them.[85] You can enjoy natural health by using the discovery that every sickness, disease, and ailment could be traced to a mineral deficiency (Pauling, 1986). This will safeguard your immune system that has the power to heal almost every illness without external medication.

Seven decades ago, as part of an investigation into American farming practices, Senate Document 264 revealed: Foods grown on millions of acres of land no longer contain enough minerals and are starving us. Quietly hidden from the public all these years, this alarming study also found that 99% of North Americans had serious nutritional deficiencies. Today, modern agricultural methods have virtually eliminated nature's most important nutrient delivery carrier, fulvic acid, which helps transport more minerals, enzymes and oxygen to the cells. The result? Millions of people with degenerative diseases.[86]

Returning to unprocessed foods closest to their natural state will supercharge the immune system to protect against disease. Super immunity can be best defined as the body's immune system working to its fullest potential. The right raw materials and nutritional factors can double or triple the protective power of the immune system. When the body's defences take on superhero qualities,

---

[84] http://tinyurl.com/alive-com-health

[85] http://tinyurl.com/imgt-org-ImmuneSystem-pdf

[86] http://tinyurl.com/biologicaltherapeutics-com-pdf

you will hardly ever get sick again. More important, this change from average immunity to super immunity can save your life.[87]

Returning to unprocessed natural foods rich with minerals for supercharging your immune system is easy: Don't eat what your mother used to cook; eat what your grandmother used to cook when there were no supermarkets selling processed food loaded with so-called 'permitted' chemical additives.

h. Problem with processed food

Traditional food processing had two functions: to make food more digestible and available during times of scarcity. This produced old-fashioned sausages, meat puddings, sourdough bread, fermented grain products, cheese and other fermented milk products, pickles, sauerkraut, and beverages such as wine, spirits and lacto-fermented soft drinks. Traditional processing enhances the nutritional value of foods. Traditional bread-making neutralises anti-nutrients in grains to make the minerals more available; lacto-fermentation of cabbage to make sauerkraut increases the levels of vitamin C and many B vitamins many fold; making yoghurt, kefir and similar products from fresh milk makes the nutrients in the milk more available and more digestible.

In a presentation at the annual conference of Consumer Health of Canada in March 2002, Sally Fallon exposed many 'dirty secrets of the food processing industry'. Modern food processing actually destroys the nutrients in food rather than increasing them, and makes food more difficult to digest. For example, studies in the 1930's and 1940's showed the superiority of raw milk over pasteurised milk in building strong bones, healthy organs and a strong nervous system. However, many people, particularly children, cannot tolerate the processed stuff called milk sold on the grocery shelves. When you use reduced-fat powdered milk thinking that it will help you avoid heart disease, you are actually consuming oxidised cholesterol that contributes to the build-up of plaque in the arteries and initiates the process of heart disease. Oranges are a very heavily sprayed crop. Modern processing that puts them in vats and squeezes them with their peel adds cancer-causing compounds to orange juice. Industrial processing depends on products and processes that have a negative

---

[87] http://tinyurl.com/jentanbernardus

impact on our health, such as sugar, white flour, processed and hydrogenated oils, additives, synthetic vitamins, and extrusion processing of grains. [88]

We often eat whole-grain breakfast cereals thinking they are healthy. The problem is not the whole grains themselves, but how they're processed in the factory. In his book, 'Fighting the Food Giants', Paul Stitt says that the extrusion process used for breakfast cereals destroys most of the nutrients in the grains. It destroys the fatty acids. It even destroys the chemical vitamins that are added at the end. The amino acids are rendered very toxic by this process. This is how all the boxed cereals are made, even the ones sold in the health food stores. In an experiment with rats conducted by a cereal company, which was unpublished for obvious reasons, rats whose diet included plain whole wheat lived over a year, while those given puffed wheat (an extruded cereal) died within two weeks from dysfunction of the pancreas, liver and kidneys and degeneration of the nerves of the spine – all signs of insulin shock.[89] Wouldn't this be the reason why diabetes has now reached epidemic proportions and is considered a lifelong disease?

With so many people eating breakfast cereals, you might expect to find some studies on the effect of extruded cereals on animals or humans. Yet, there are no published studies at all in the scientific literature. It's worth noting that cereals are a multi-billion dollar business, one that has created huge fortunes. The only advances made in the extrusion process are those that will cut costs, regardless of how these will alter the nutrient content of the end product.

i. Benefits of an alkalising diet

Everything that we eat or drink leaves either an acidic or alkaline residue after digestion. For example, lemons are acidic, but have an alkalising effect on the body after digestion; milk is alkaline, but becomes acidic after digestion. The pH scale used to measure the acidity or alkalinity of any substance ranges from 0 (acidic) to 14 (alkaline), with 7 as neutral. Below 7 is increasingly acidic. Above 7 is increasingly alkaline. Human life requires a tightly controlled, slightly alkaline pH level in the blood of about 7.4 (7.35 to 7.45). When it comes to the pH level and the net acid load in the human diet, there has been considerable deterioration from the hunter-gatherer civilisation to the modern

[88] http://www.roseofsharonfarm.com/Dirty%20Secrets.pdf

[89] http://tinyurl.com/members-chello-nl-Food-pdf

day. Much has been written on the benefits of an alkaline diet for staying naturally healthy.[90]

When your body tends to become overly acidic (due to food and lifestyle choices, environment, chemicals, etc.) your body will 'steal' alkalising minerals like calcium, magnesium, and potassium from your bones, teeth, and organs to neutralise the acids. Robbing your body reserves over time can lead to osteoporosis and higher risk of cancer, heart disease and arthritis. Excess acidity in the body can interfere with the digestive system, liver, kidneys, and our ability to fight viruses and bad bacteria like yeast and fungus. Excess acidity can cause inflammation, allergies, skin problems, constipation, bowel issues and stress (both physical & mental). An alkaline diet (fresh fruits, leafy greens, wheatgrass, raw vegetables, sprouts, green juices, etc.) as opposed to an acidic diet (high in animal products, processed carbs, refined sugar, energy drinks, etc.) floods our bodies with chlorophyll, vitamins and minerals.[91]

Researchers have found that many people in our modern society are too acid, due to excessive consumption of sugars, grains, animal protein and legal drugs. Signs of high acidity include fatigue, getting out of breath easily, and frequent muscle pain/cramping. They recommend eating more alkali-producing foods and less acid-producing foods, in a ratio of about three to one.[92]

j. Acidic vs. alkaline food

Figure 5 depicts an acidic-alkaline food chart, which can guide your choice of what to eat and drink. Though there are some differences in similar charts from different sources, their contents are broadly similar. What you find on the left side are wholesome raw foods that are cheaper to buy than those on the right side. Contrary to common belief, cooking does not remove the agrochemical residues found in farmed vegetables. Eating them raw will help the body's natural ability to get rid of such chemical residues. The fresh fruits and raw vegetables you consume should ideally be organically grown and eaten in their natural form, instead of drinking their juice. As you can see, almost

[90] http://www.ncbi.nlm.nih.gov/pmc/articles/PMC3195546/

[91] http://kriscarr.com/blog-video/ph-balance-alkaline-foods/

[92] http://tinyurl.com/math-ucsd-edu-FoodAcidity

everything we consume daily is on the acidic side. This could be one reason why we are getting sicker instead of healthier.

We need to balance what we eat and drink from the right side of the food chart with what is on the left side. For example, if you love to drink bubbly beer, balance it with something alkaline (like breast milk!). To meet the 3 to 1 ratio mentioned earlier, 75% of what you consume should come from the left (alkaline) side and 25% from the right (acidic) side.

Most Alkaline	**Alkaline**	**Least Alkaline**	**FOOD CATEGORY**	**Least Acid**	**Acid**	**Most Acid**
	Maple Syrup, Rice Syrup	Raw Honey, Raw Sugar	SWEETENERS	Processed Honey, Molasses	White Sugar, Brown Sugar	NutraSweet, Equal, Aspartame, Sweet 'N Low
Lemons, Limes, Watermelon, Grapefruit, Mangoes, Papayas	Dates, Figs, Melons, Grapes, Kiwi, Apples, Pears, Raisins	Oranges, Bananas, Cherries, Pineapples, Peaches, Avocados	FRUITS	Plums, Processed Fruit Juices	Rhubarb	Blackberries, Cranberries, Prunes
Asparagus, Onions, Garlic, Raw Vegetables, Parsley, Raw Spinach, Broccoli	Okra, Squash, Green Beans, Beets, Celery, Lettuce, Zucchini, Sweet Potatoes, Carob	Carrots, Tofu, Tomatoes, Fresh Corn, Cabbage, Mushrooms, Peas, Potato Skins, Olives, Soybeans	BEANS & VEGETABLES	Cooked Spinach, Kidney Beans, String Beans	Potatoes (without skins), Pinto Beans, Navy Beans, Lima Beans	Chocolate
	Almonds	Chestnuts	NUTS & SEEDS	Pumpkin Seeds, Sunflower Seeds	Pecans, Cashews	Peanuts, Walnuts
Olive Oil	Flax Seed Oil	Canola Oil	OILS	Corn Oil		
		Amaranth, Millet, Wild Rice	GRAINS & CEREALS	Brown Rice	White Rice, Corn, Oats, Rye	White Flour, Wheat, Pasta, Pastries
			FISH & MEAT	Venison, Fish	Turkey, Lamb, Chicken	Beef, Pork, Shellfish
	Breast Milk	Soya Cheese, Soya Milk, Whey, Goat Milk, Goat Cheese	EGGS & DAIRY	Eggs, Butter, Yogurt, Buttermilk, Cottage Cheese	Raw Milk	Cheese, Homogenized Milk, Ice Cream
Herb Teas, Lemon Water	Green Tea	Ginger Tea	BEVERAGES	Tea	Coffee	Beer, Soft Drinks

Figure 5. Alkaline vs. Acidic Foods
Source: http://www.billschoolcraft.com/ph/

k. How I stay naturally healthy

Based on what has been presented so far, here is how I have managed to stay naturally healthy over the past decades without using any medicines:

1. Every morning, drink a glass of lukewarm water with freshly-squeezed juice from half a lime or quarter lemon on an empty stomach, and wait at least 10 minutes before eating. This alkalises your body, helps you detoxify, improves your digestion and boosts your metabolism & energy levels.[93]
2. Every day, drink several cups of leaf green tea (tea bags are too small to contain high-quality leaf green tea). Green tea provides many health benefits such as: killing bacteria and lowering risk of infections; improving dental and general health, brain function, fat-burning and physical performance; reducing risk of cancer, cardiovascular disease, type II diabetes, Alzheimer's, Parkinson's and obesity.[94]
3. Avoid all forms of processed food & beverages, and consume organic items whenever possible.
4. Eat and drink 75% of alkaline foods (e.g. fresh fruits and raw vegetables) and only 25% of acidic foods as shown in Figure 5.
5. Chew each mouthful until it becomes a liquid, while counting to ensure chewing at least 32 times. Even liquids should be 'chewed' to ensure pre-digestion in the mouth.
6. Eat a lot of greens (ideally raw) to enable their chlorophyll to oxygenate the cells in the body.
7. Intersperse stress-producing mental activities with short breaks at least every two hours to relax eyes (e.g. aimlessly looking out through a window), mind and body (using the techniques described earlier).
8. Do some physical activity every day (walking, dancing, sports, taking the stairs instead of lift, etc.).
9. Drink enough water, whenever feeling thirsty. In case of constipation, try drinking more water.
10. Not smoking (destroys the internal 'pranic' energy), and taking only a minimum of alcohol (no more than a glass of red wine per day – good for the heart, but not for the brain).

---

[93] http://www.truthaboutabs.com/drink-this.html#13;&

[94] http://tinyurl.com/authoritynutrition-comGreenTea

11. Deep abdominal breathing to maximise the intake of oxygen with each breath.
12. Live an intense but enjoyable life every day, with enough relaxation and sleep.
13. Spend time with people who willingly follow the health habits mentioned above.

The main idea is to take personal responsibility for healing your illnesses through the Hippocrates diet, deep breathing to oxygenate the cells and boost your immune system, and commanding your subconscious mind to heal you, which is the basis of energy medicine.

I. Energy medicine

The body's energies are the key to health, vitality, and well-being. Energy medicine is the practice of correcting health issues through the body's energy system, which allows the body's immune system to do its healing work unhindered. This immune response contributes to homeostasis, which is the auto-correction process that enables the body to maintain normal, healthy ranges for things like temperature, energy intake and growth. Energy medicine is the art and science of helping people to clear blockages and develop their body energies to live happier, healthier and more fulfilling lives.[95]

According to a Stanford University Medical School research released in 1998 by Dr. Bruce Lipton, stress is the cause of at least 95% of all illness and disease. Too much stress for too long creates what is known as 'chronic stress' which has been linked to heart disease, stroke, and may also influence cancer and chronic respiratory diseases. That's because chronic stress turns off the effectiveness of your immune system that can heal just about any health problem.[96]

Stress typically originates from beliefs about us and our interpretation of circumstances as threatening. When we feel threatened, the cells in our body get mobilised into a fight or flight mode, as opposed to a normal, healthy growth mode. A continuation of such battle readiness over time will drain body energy and lead to illness and disease. We cannot have disease without

[95] http://www.energymed.org/

[96] http://www.lpgmindworks.com/newsletters/september2010stressndisease.html

first having an energetic disturbance in the cells and organs, rendering our body energy flow ineffective.[97]

Two techniques based on energy medicine that can help you to heal yourself are summarised below.

m. Healing Codes (6-minute antidote to stress)

In 2001, Dr. Alex Loyd (a naturopathic Doctor with a PhD in Psychology) discovered a previously undiscovered de-stressing mechanism in the body.[98] He discovered a way to teach normal individuals how to bring their bodies from scientifically diagnosed out-of-balance stress levels to in-balance levels within 20 minutes using self-applied exercises. He found that when you remove the destructive images in the heart and subsequently remove stress from the body, the neuro-immune system can heal just about any disease or any physical problem on its own.

The Healing Codes system, by focusing on the destructive pictures in the heart and eliminating them, is able to heal the stress and the wrong beliefs that underlie the physical and nonphysical problems that afflict people. It heals by changing the underlying destructive energy pattern or frequency of the image to a healthy one. The Healing Codes system works without conscious awareness of the destructive images, beliefs, thoughts and feelings that are being healed. These are collectively located in four locations on the neck and head. When these areas are showered with healthy energy, such energy spreads to the destructive images stored in the body/mind, and positively affects the physiology of the body. This is done by bringing together the tips of the thumbs and four fingers of each hand into two little circles and pointing them at the four locations on the neck and head in sequence, to emit a stream of healthy energy that flows from all areas of the body.

When you do the Healing Codes with the appropriate combination of the four healing centres, you are literally showering every cell in the body with healing energy. The healing centres are:

1. Bridge position, located between the two eyebrows;
2. Adam's apple position, at the base of your throat;

---

[97] http://www.electrical-sensitivity.info/HealingCodesReport.pdf

[98] http://thehealingcodeinfo.com/EXCERPT-vbt.PDF

3. Jaw position, at the bottom back corners of your jawbones under each ear;
4. Temples position, at the outside of the two eyes.

These four healing centres are energised in the above sequence for about 20 seconds each by aiming the pointed tips of all fingers in each hand about 5-7 cm away from each healing centre, for a total of about 6 minutes (5 complete cycles).

Having the fingertips this distance away from each healing centre creates an energy field that allows the body to automatically produce the precise positive/negative energy pattern needed for healing. This process is accompanied by your wish/prayer that all your physical issues and their causes are healed through love and divine/cosmic light.
For a detailed explanation, visit: http://www.thehealingcode.com/lssr.html
For a demonstration, visit: https://www.youtube.com/watch?v=Y1Vk1fIODAk

n. Tapping (Emotional Freedom Technique – EFT)

Founded on discoveries in 1980 by the psychologist Dr. Roger Callahan and subsequently refined by Gary Craig, EFT is based on the discovery that imbalances in the body's energy system have profound effects on one's psychology and physiology. Correcting these imbalances, which is done by tapping on certain body locations, often provides a rapid remedy. The method consists of combining Western talk therapy with the Oriental acupressure technique of tapping with the fingertips at the end points of the body's energy meridians. Tapping provides relief from chronic pain, emotional problems, disorders, addictions, phobias, post-traumatic stress disorder, and physical diseases.[99] A summarised version of EFT is given below. For a detailed explanation, visit: https://www.thrivingnow.com/eft-tapping-points/

Identify the problem you want to focus on. It can be general anxiety, or it can be a specific situation or issue which causes you to feel anxious. Then, rate the intensity level of your anxiety, from zero being the lowest level to ten being the highest. Compose a set up statement that acknowledges the problem you want to deal with, followed by an unconditional affirmation of yourself as a person. For example: *Even though I have this ...., I deeply and completely*

[99] https://www.youtube.com/watch?v=VFKVVP8KXd4

accept myself, where you fill in the blank with whatever problem you want to address and resolve (e.g. fear of public speaking, headache, backache, breathing difficulty, depression, craving for alcohol, frequent anger, financial problem, etc.). While saying your above set up statement three times aloud, using the fingertips of four fingers of one hand, tap the 'karate chop' point on the other hand as shown in Figure 6.

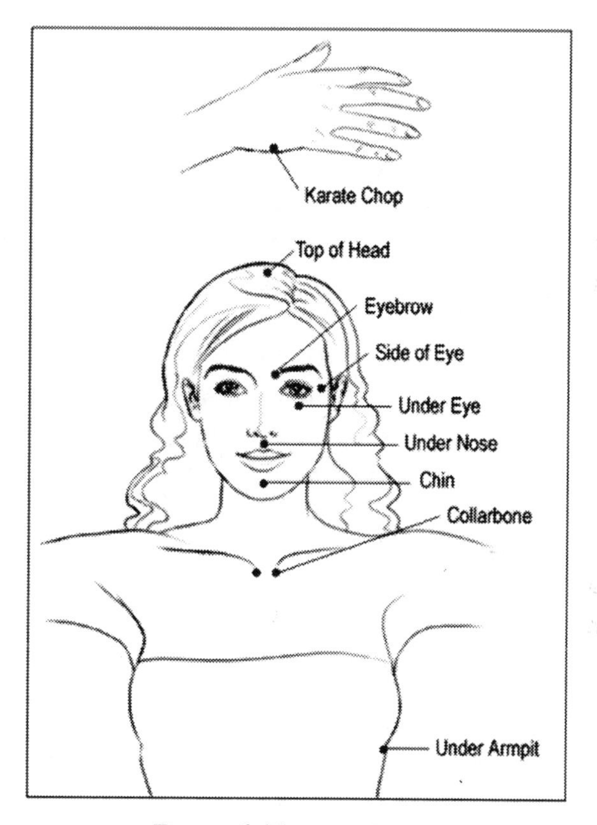

Figure 6. Tapping Points

Then, using the fingertips (not nails) of the index and middle fingers, firmly but gently tap 5 to 7 times each of the eight tapping points (see Figure 6) on one side of your face in the following sequence, while using a reminder phrase such as: *My fear of public speaking*:

1. *Top of head* (tap with the tips of four fingers).
2. *Eyebrow* (inner edge of an eyebrow, close to bridge of the nose).
3. *Side of eye* (hard bony ridge between the eye and the temple).

4. *Under eye* (hard area under the eye).
5. *Under nose* (between the bottom of the nose and the upper lip).
6. *Chin* (halfway between the bottom of the lower lip and the chin).
7. *Collarbone* (tap with a loose fist on the breastbone).
8. *Underarm* (tap with the tips of four fingers about four inches or ten centimetres beneath the armpit).
9. *Top of head* (same as before).

If, after doing one such round, your anxiety is still high (say about public speaking), repeat the tapping sequence until it is completely gone or it is very low when compared to your rating when you started. After that, repeat the tapping sequence while making a positive and empowering affirmation with emotion about that specific issue (for example: *I love to speak in front of a group*). Don't state positive affirmations using negative expressions such as: *I have no fear of public speaking.*

Through this simple approach, EFT enables you to first accept and deal with a specific anxiety or negative feeling, after which, you create positive and healing thoughts. For a demonstration of EFT by its founder Gary Craig, visit: https://www.youtube.com/watch?v=1wG2FA4vfLQ

9. Developing Wisdom and Skills

Sports-related competencies alone
are not enough to win matches

Developing the six dimensions of success is parallel to improving the different competencies needed to excel in any sport. For example, to excel in tennis, you need to have a very good serve, forehand and back hand groundstrokes, and the ability to lob, smash, volley and play cross-court, down-the-line and drop shots very well. However, this alone will not ensure a win in a competitive situation. Why is that?

Wayne Gretzky, considered the greatest ice hockey player ever, provides some important insights. When he began his NHL (National Hockey League of Canada) career at 18, he stood 6 ft (183 cm) tall and weighed 160 pounds (73 kg). Many critics claimed that he was 'too small, too wiry, and too slow to be a force in the NHL.' Realising that he was not naturally gifted in terms of physical size and skating speed, he had to work hard for his successes. He found that 90% of ice hockey was mental. He attributes his phenomenal success to his uncanny ability to skate to where the puck is going to be, not where it has been.[100] In other words, while other players were chasing behind the puck, he 'knew' what to do next.

9.1 Wisdom-Skills competency matrix

In almost everything we do in life, success appears to depend on two decisive factors: Wisdom – knowing what to do next, and Skills – knowing how to

[100] http://michaelmindes.com/wisdom-wayne-gretzky-quotes

do it (definitions by the American ichthyologist, David Starr Jordan). The wisdom-skills competency matrix shown in Figure 7 broadly identifies the competencies as well as the associated training needs for achieving success in any field of human endeavour: sports, music, arts, writing, medicine, architecture, engineering, business, finance, etc.

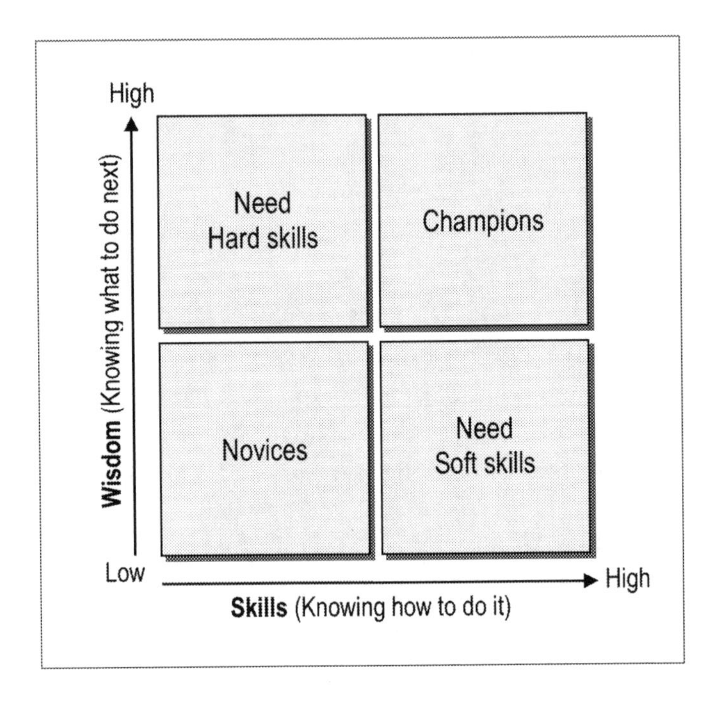

Figure 7. Wisdom-Skills Competency Matrix©
Source: My conceptualisation[101]

In the wisdom-skills competency matrix shown in Figure 7, Wisdom stems from a mix of insights gained through inner soft skills (personal insights gained through mindfulness), outer soft skills (insights gained through others), and work-related hard skills. Skills relate mainly to work-related hard skills tempered with insights gained through soft skills. Without wisdom, a person or organisation could strive to address wrong issues and solve irrelevant problems. Without skills, a person or organisation will not be able to do what needs to be done.

---

101 http://tinyurl.com/aabss-org-au-5Dimensions-pdf

The wisdom-skills matrix also provides a broad framework for identifying individual training needs. Individuals who are high on wisdom but low on skills are typically older people who need training in relevant hard skills (e.g. computer skills). Individuals who are low on wisdom but high on skills tend to be newly-qualified younger people, who need more work experience and training in both inner and outer soft skills. People who are low on both wisdom and skills could be novices who need training in both hard and soft skills, or people whose interests lie outside their current areas of work.

Becoming a Champion with fully developed hard and soft skills should be your aim as a highflyer. As a Champion, you will become a powerful change agent, who can lift others to champion level through your high levels of personal motivation and engagement. This will happen as you develop your Heart, Mind, Passion and Focus dimensions, supported by Body and Health dimensions.

9.2 Intuitive wisdom

Rational knowledge and practical experience are key components of our skills. However, while these can consolidate the present, they do not have the power to create your future, which requires wisdom founded on intuitive insights. Such insights cannot be obtained only through analysis or wilful concentration. They tend to appear suddenly, not when one is working but when relaxing with an empty mind (Heider, 1986).

There are two systems that drive the way we think and make choices. One system is fast, intuitive and emotional, while the other is slower, more deliberate and logical. Fast thinking has extraordinary capabilities and also faults and biases, while intuitive impressions have a strong influence on our thoughts and behaviour. Most impressions and thoughts arise in our conscious mind without us knowing how they got there. The mental work that produces intuitions, impressions and decisions happens unobtrusively in our mind. There is nothing magical about intuition since we all perform feats of intuitive expertise many times each day. The confidence we have in our intuitive beliefs and preferences is usually justified, but not always, since we tend to be confident even when we are wrong (Kahneman, 2011).

a. Knowing without thinking

Have you noticed those moments when you instinctively 'know' something without knowing why? This phenomenon called 'blink' produces snap judgements that could often be more effective than a cautious, rational decision. This is the power of 'thinking without thinking' by our subconscious mind, which can quickly process a lot of data for sizing up complex situations, warn us of danger, and initiate necessary action in a simple manner. For example, by trusting their instincts, an art expert sees a ten-million-dollar sculpture and instantly spots it's a fake; a fire-fighter suddenly senses he has to get out of a blazing building which was about to collapse (Gladwell, 2005). Animals do this instinctively. During the tsunami that struck Sri Lanka in 2004, very few animals died while thousands of people lost their lives.

This ability of our subconscious mind to find patterns in situations and behaviour, based on very narrow slices of experience, is called thin-slicing in psychology and philosophy.[102] It appears to have the ability to sift through any situation, throw out all that is irrelevant, and zero-in on what really matters to the point that thin-slicing can sometimes deliver a better answer than more deliberate and exhaustive ways of thinking. However, despite all its power, our subconscious mind is fallible. Our instinctive reactions can be thrown off, distracted or disabled as a result of having to compete with other interests, emotions and sentiments.

b. Downloading wisdom

During periods of relaxation after concentrated intellectual activity, the intuitive mind seems to take over and produce sudden flashes of clarifying insights into what needs to be done to achieve a desired goal. When the rational mind is silenced, the intuitive mode produces an extraordinary awareness where fragmented perceptions of reality blend into a holistic unity. In this heightened state of awareness, one is neither tense nor hurried, but filled with mental energy that can be channelled to reach any desired goal, no matter how daunting (Capra, 1983).

Our intuition is like our cosmic connection to the universe, through which we receive flashes of inspiration and intuitional insights. By calming and developing our Mind dimension, we can learn to strengthen our cosmic connection and increase its 'bandwidth' to 'download' creative ideas and

---

[102] http://www.innovateus.net/innopedia/what-term-thin-slicing

innovative solutions to any complex problem (Del Pe, 2006). You also need communication skills to convey your ideas to others effectively and efficiently.

9.3 Communication skills

Research has shown that up to 55% of human communication occurs through nonverbal expressions (including body language, gestures, how we dress, behave, etc.), and a further 38% through paralanguage (nonverbal communication such as tone of voice, laughter, gestures, facial expressions, etc. that accompany speech and convey further meaning).[103] This means that only about 7% of what we try to communicate is conveyed purely through the words we use.

a. How to connect with people

You have to connect before you can communicate. You connect with people when you are using the same communication frequency of body and mind. Observing and matching voice and mannerisms that enables you to connect with people is an instinctive process that takes place mostly at the subconscious level. All what you learnt about body language will probably get in your way if you start thinking about it. Even matching the content of your conversation (such as giving too much or too little information) should be based on your ability to sense if you are holding or losing the interest of your listener. The primary driver of this communication process is your Heart dimension fed by your Passion and Focus dimensions, with some help from the Mind dimension.

b. How to communicate effectively

Firstly, this requires genuine interest in the other person and what he or she is trying to communicate.

Secondly, it requires non-judgemental listening so you are hearing what they are actually saying instead of your interpretation of what you think they are saying filtered through your own thoughts and beliefs.

Thirdly, it requires relaxed concentration that enables you to look for the subtext underlying their spoken words before you start formulating your

[103] https://en.wikipedia.org/wiki/Communication

responses. Good communication requires that you 'listen' to how the listener is listening to you.

The survival of tribal societies depended on close communication and rapport between their members. A proverb that dates back to the Cherokee tribe of Native Americans says: *Don't judge a man until you have walked a mile in his shoes.*[104] This requires you to take off your own shoes (meaning your preconceptions, prejudices, etc.) when trying to communicate with another person, which requires non-judgemental awareness.

In written communication, you can only use words. Words have great power. We can use words to create visions and feelings. Just like when speaking, the words you use should depend on the person you are writing to, and geared to achieving your communication objective. Written communication requires a mix of Heart and Mind dimensions supported by the Focus dimension. Guidance for written communication can be downloaded from websites such as: http://tinyurl.com/acquaint-me-uk-Written-pdf

We use verbal communication to make our *meaning* understood through word order and phrasing (syntax) combined with word choice and meaning (semantics). To hold the attention of a listener, use simple words and short sentences. A good general rule is to mimic the listener's volume and speech rate, both of which help you to build rapport, which is an essential ingredient of good communication. It's a matter of being sensitive to a listener's reaction, and matching your own volume and speech rate accordingly. Verbal communication is related to our Mind dimension. When the mind is clear, thoughts and words are clear.

We use nonverbal communication to make our *attitude* understood, often at a subconscious level. Much of our communication is not so much in *what* we say, but in *how* we say it. Are we standing in a self-assured yet non-threatening way? Are we maintaining a comfortable level of eye contact? Are we engaging the listener with our gestures? Adjust your approach based on your observations of your listener and your understanding of the situation. Non-verbal communication is related to our Heart dimension. When you feel empathy towards your listener, you will project warmth and concern and your non-verbal communication will become naturally easy.

When you're talking on the telephone, you are unable to confirm visually to what extent the listener has your attention. Therefore, the sounds you make,

---

104 http://tinyurl.com/planetofsuccess-com-Empathy

rather than spoken words, such as *uh-huh, ahh,* and *umm* will communicate that you're listening and actively engaged. Also, when communicating over the phone, the tone and volume of your voice convey a lot of information nonverbally.[105]

In any conversation, we mostly communicate the underlying mental and emotional energy. For example, if you dislike a person, no matter how politely you speak, he or she will subconsciously pickup your negative feelings. Conversely, if you want to make friends with someone you rather dislike but have to work with, you can mentally project the thought and feeling that you like that person.

c. How to influence others

The first step in influencing others is connecting with them and aligning their minds with the direction of your thoughts. You find a beautiful example of this in the film Avatar. Before the native Na'vi people can ride any creature in their world, they have to connect the tip of their long braided hair to the antennae that all creatures have. This connection enables Na'vi riders to connect with their mounts mentally and use minimal physical effort to guide their actions.[106]

Here are some techniques based on those presented by Yumi Sakugawa that will get people to do what you want:[107]

1. Be charming, confident and likeable since people will tend to do what you want if they like you.
2. Mirror their verbal and nonverbal behaviour to build rapport and trust.
3. Making a person say 'yes' or nod or agree with what you say will make his or her subconscious mind more receptive to whatever you say afterwards.
4. Make the person feel respected and important since everyone loves to feel they are special.
5. Use your words to tap into a person's imagination to create positive images and feelings about what you are suggesting, since emotional appeals work better than rational appeals for most people.

---

105 http://tinyurl.com/saylor-org-Communication-pdf

106 http://james-camerons-avatar.wikia.com/wiki/Queue

107 http://tinyurl.com/thesecretyumiverse-WonderHowTo

6. Inspire people to do what is required, as opposed to telling them what to do.
7. Sincerely show that you have the person's best interests at heart.

Your ability to persuade others governs your ability to resolve conflicts.

d. How to resolve conflicts

The key to resolving conflicts is found in what Niels Bohr (pioneering quantum physicist and winner of Nobel Prize in Physics in 1922) has said: *The opposite of a trivial truth is plainly false. The opposite of a great truth is also true.*[108] Conflicts arise when different people see different aspects of the same reality using their different points of view. As Albert Einstein has said: *We cannot solve our problems with the same thinking we used when we created them.*[109] Therefore, we have to use a higher level of thinking to resolve conflicts. For resolving conflicts, you need to use your Heart, Mind and Focus dimensions.

Start by finding a high level concept that the opposing parties would all agree to, in a cooperative setting in a non-judgemental manner. For example, let's say that the father (who is authoritarian) and the mother (who is lenient) of a child have conflicting views on how to bring up their child. The starting point in the conflict resolution process would be a casual discussion to guide their thinking to a future scenario where their child will have to fight to succeed in a fiercely competitive world. Then, help them to think of the best way to empower their child and develop its self-confidence. During this process, they will discover to what extent their two approaches would support or oppose the agreed goal of empowering their child to overcome complex challenges on its own.

This process involves an open discussion about the pros and cons of their different approaches in order to find the most viable solution to reach the agreed higher level goal. This usually would be a mix of their different approaches. Once you help the opposing parties to communicate freely and openly, the opposing parties will resolve their conflict on their own and take joint responsibility for implementing the agreed course of action. This won't happen if you resolve their conflict.

---

[108] http://www.brainyquote.com/quotes/quotes/n/nielsbohr165246.html

[109] http://www.brainyquote.com/quotes/quotes/a/alberteins121993.html

Part Four:

Using Your Flying Skills

10. Getting Ready to Fly

Flying skills are of little use
unless you are willing to fly high and far

Many birds are hemmed in by the Himalayas. But not bar-headed geese. They are the highest flying birds in the world. They fly over the Himalayas where the air is dangerously thin. They suffer severe hypoxia and the resulting pain due to insufficient oxygen reaching the tissues, probably way beyond any human athlete.[110] The Arctic tern holds the long-distance migration record for birds, travelling between Arctic breeding grounds and the Antarctic each year. This is equal to each bird flying to the moon and back three times during its life.[111] Bird migration carries high costs in predation and mortality, including hunting by humans. Despite the risks involved, all these birds symbolise the joy of flying higher and further than everyone else.

10.1 How to find flying companions

You fly alone. However, having people around you who love to fly will motivate you to fly to unprecedented heights. Jim Rohn has said, *You are the average of the five people you spend the most time with.*[112] The people around you affect you consciously and subconsciously. They influence your thinking, attitudes and behaviours, and the level of success you aim for.

General Colin Powell explained this clearly: *'The less you associate with some people, the more your life will improve. An important attribute in successful people*

---

[110] https://www.youtube.com/watch?v=WnNQWj98BR0

[111] https://www.youtube.com/watch?v=bte7MCSBZvo

[112] http://tinyurl.com/lifehacker-com-Success

is their impatience with negative thinking and negative acting people. As you grow, your associates will change. Some of your friends will not want you to go on. They will want you to stay where they are. Friends that don't help you climb will want you to crawl.[113] What if you don't know people of a high calibre to associate with? Here are three things you can do:

1. When you come across such people, find a way to associate with them by making them realise that you share their high aspirations.
2. When dealing with people who are not yet at that level, treat them with care and respect, but don't connect with them mentally and emotionally. You can do this by looking at them and hearing what they say in a detached manner, while guarding your thoughts and emotions from anything negative they are saying. For example, when watching a television program that disturbs you, focussing your attention on the frame of the television will mentally detach you from its content.
3. What if you can't find people who can motivate you to fly higher? Make yourself your flying companion. Develop an internal dialogue with yourself to evaluate your progress and cheer yourself on, despite any setbacks. This happens only when you totally love and accept yourself unconditionally, and let your inner wisdom guide you. This has been my approach because I couldn't find people who shared my dreams of achieving the highest levels of success.

10.2 How to profile people quickly

Say you meet a person who looks like a good flying companion for you. Can you 'read' and profile such a person quickly in a nonintrusive and discrete manner? You can do this very quickly, by using the six dimensional model: Heart: can you 'feel' this person and connect with her or him easily? Mind: do you feel from what he or she is saying that he or she is intelligent and wise? Passion: do you feel her or his energy? Focus: is he or she attentive despite distractions?

---

[113] http://tinyurl.com/goodreads-com-ColinPowell

Body: does she or he seem to be taking good care of her or his body? Health: if she or he looks healthy, ask what she or he is doing to look so healthy. You can use the answers to these six questions to profile a person discretely in a matter of minutes. These could be prospective flying companions, or people you have to deal with on the way to reaching your goals.

11. Where to Fly: Selecting Goals

Check if a goal is worth the effort
before taking off and not after landing

Once you know how to fly with your mind using all the flying skills you have developed, you can reach any goal. How can you identify goals that are meaningful to you? Rather than selecting goals in an unplanned manner, a good starting point would be to see how well balanced your life is.

11.1 How balanced is your life?

The universe is an orderly and stable system that is in a state of dynamic balance despite the ever-changing nature of all things. Similarly, when your life is well balanced, you live in a harmonious manner. This means different things to different people. If your life is unbalanced, you will have little pockets of unhappiness that show themselves from time to time and disturb your peace of mind.

Here is a simple way to check if all the different aspects of your life are balanced, when seen from your own personal perspective.

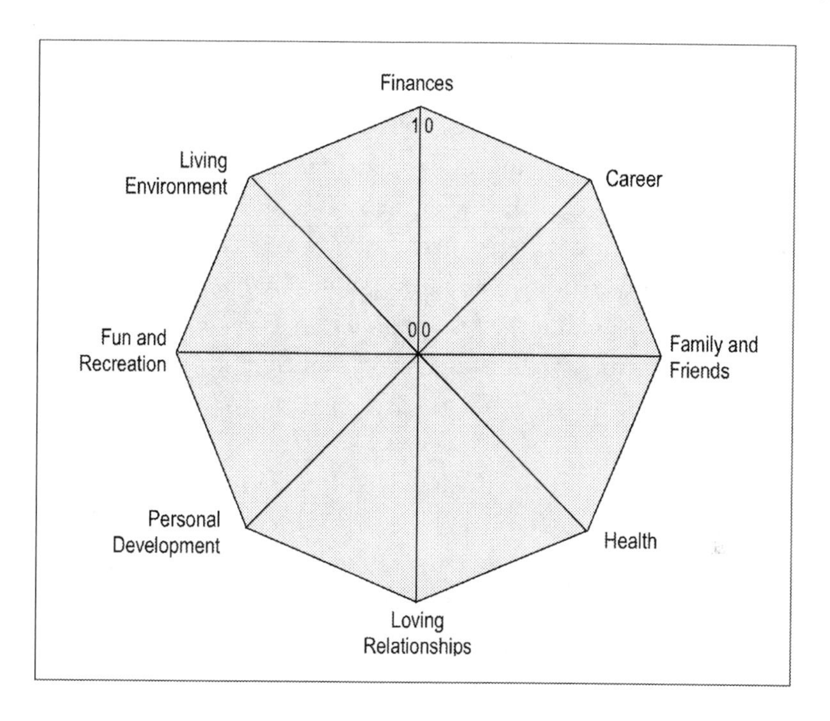

Figure 8. The wheel of life
Source: Adapted from the work of David Jemitus[114]

For each of the eight segments shown in Figure 8, give yourself a rating between 0 and 10, where 0 means you don't have anything, and 10 means you have everything you want. On the line representing each segment, place a dot that shows the rating you have given for that segment. For example, if your health is not too good and not too bad, rate it at 5 and place a dot halfway on the line for health. When you finish doing this, each line will have a dot that represents your rating for that segment. Now connect the dots on the lines next to each other using straight lines. You will end up with a wheel that gives you a pictorial representation of how the 8 different aspects of your life are balanced relative to each other.

Ideally, you should have a balanced wheel close to that shown in Figure 8, where each of the 8 aspects has a high rating. Any low ratings you have given will identify the areas that need improvement. In each such area, think of a major goal you would like to achieve.

---

114 http://www.davidjemitus.name/whatislifeallabout.html

11.2 Aim for unrealistic goals

Seemingly unrealistic goals are easier to achieve than realistic goals. This is because reaching for an unusually challenging goal is exciting enough to produce a burst of adrenaline. You need that to help you overcome the inevitable challenges and sufferings that accompany the achievement of any seemingly unrealistic goal, such as creating a new life just the way you want. Realistic goals that lie within the average ambition level are uninspiring. These will only fuel you through the first or second challenge, after which you would throw in the towel. If the potential payoff is mediocre or average, so would be your effort (Ferris, 2007).

On the other hand, a goal called a BHAG (pronounced bee-hag) stands for a Bold, Hair-raising, Audacious Goal that you set for yourself. Something the sheer thought of which excites you and makes you want to step outside your comfort zone and stretch yourself to achieve it – an exciting goal at the edge of your current reach that would be great to achieve if you can somehow mobilise the necessary skills, resources, etc. My personal BHAG is to win the Oscar for the best foreign film for my next feature film that my subconscious mind is busy working on and sending me flashes of storyline, dialogue and images.

If this book were about the 'realistic' goal of achieving a higher level of success in your life, instead of the 'unrealistic' goal of creating miracles in your life, would you still have bought it? Would you have the motivation to practise the simple but powerful techniques explained in it for flying to dizzy heights, and achieving ambitious goals you never even dreamt of?

11.3 How to select your goals

What do you want to do to balance your life in ways that would blow your mind? This mindset will help you identify exciting goals that are also meaningful from a holistic view of your life. Here is a simple process that can get you started. Depending on how you have marked each of the eight areas in your wheel of life (Figure 8), use the table below to identify a specific, ambitious goal you wish to achieve within a specific time period (say 12 months) in each area that needs your attention. Try to make each one a BHAG.

Finances:	
Career:	
Family & Friends:	
Health:	
Loving Relationships:	
Personal Development:	
Fun & Recreation:	
Living Environment:	

Having done that for each applicable area, use the right column to prioritise each one. Now you know which BHAGs to achieve in which order.

12. How to Achieve Goals

Overcoming obstacles on the way is the goal,
not the goal itself

As a highflyer, you will set your own goals and achieve them after making any necessary modifications identified during the process. You will be your own coach, mentor and counsellor during this exciting process. It leads to higher levels of personal development, which is independent of any ambitious goal you may or may not achieve during this process. A basic concept of Zen Buddhism is: *The path is the goal* (Trungpa, 2011). This means, for example, while you build a house, the house builds you. Therefore, irrespective of any outcome, developing and using your mental flying skills to reach difficult goals will empower you to take charge of your everyday life and personal development. This will lead to invaluable outcomes such as higher levels of achievement, fulfilment and consciousness.

12.1 Master the 'outer game'

Achieving goals involves all six dimensions of success to varying degrees. Most importantly, it involves an 'inner game' and an 'outer game' as explained by Timothy Gallwey in his insightful book, 'The Inner Game of Tennis', which uses tennis as an example.[115] The inner game is played against our internal adversaries such as nervousness, lack of confidence, poor concentration, fear of failure, etc., while the outer game is played against external adversaries and challenges.

115 http://tinyurl.com/tinapse

The subconscious mind is the powerhouse that can help you reach the highest levels of excellence in any sport or activity. But, it is guided by our conscious mind. In any competitive scenario, thoughts such as the fear of losing or not being able to play well will typically dominate the conscious mind. Such mental distractions interfere with the vast ability of the superfast subconscious mind to achieve exceptional levels of performance. Roger Banister became the first man to run the 4-minute mile in 1954, by ignoring the commonly-held belief that any attempt to do so will cause death by heart failure.

Novak Djokovic, after winning the men's singles tennis title easily at Wimbledon 2015, has said: *I try to put myself only in the present moment, not fight against the thoughts and the pressure and the excitement, but just acknowledge them and be aware of present thoughts but also try to keep my composure and calm. I try to just be in the moment and enjoy.*[116] Being totally in the present moment sedates the conscious mind, so the subconscious mind can get on with what needs to be done without undue interference. Understanding how the conscious and subconscious minds work will help you to win any outer game in the arena of life by winning the inner game.

12.2 Align both minds with your goals

You have one brain with two minds: conscious and subconscious. The conscious mind is responsible for logic and reasoning, and controls everything you do while you are conscious. The subconscious mind holds your beliefs, memories and emotions, and runs your entire body on autopilot by managing all your body processes such as body temperature, heartbeat, digestion, immune system, etc. The conscious mind functions like the programs we activate to perform different tasks on a computer. The subconscious mind is like the underlying invisible operating system under which all such programs function. Our antenna, which helps us to get what we desire from the external world, is connected to our subconscious mind. It has no direct connection with our conscious mind that decides what we want.

The conscious mind gives orders like the captain of a ship. If the orders are clear, the subconscious mind takes them literally and obeys them like the ship and crew, as long as those orders don't trigger contradictory beliefs relating to

---

116 http://tinyurl.com/independent-uk-wimbledon

the welfare of the ship. One study suggests that the conscious mind processes only about 2,000 bits of information per second and its impulses travel only at 100-150 mph (160-240 km/h), while the subconscious mind processes a massive 400 billion bits of information per second and its impulses zoom around at a speed of up to 100,000 mph (160,000 km/h).[117]

Goals are set by the conscious mind and achieved by the subconscious mind, as seen in all competitive sports. The conscious mind is far too slow for most fast-paced sports such as tennis, soccer, cricket, etc. Many talented sportspersons fail at the highest competitive levels, not due to any sudden loss of skill, but due to stress in the conscious mind caused by a fear of losing. This interferes with the optimum deployment of available skills by the subconscious mind. This is similar to how micromanaging capable people working under you (by closely monitoring everything they do) leads to stress, confusion, disempowerment and lower productivity.

Any conflict between the conscious and subconscious minds will hinder the achievement of any goal. For example, imagine you are trying to get a career promotion and working hard to achieve it. Any subconscious fear you have about the resulting increase in responsibility reducing the time you have to spend with your family, will prevent you from getting promoted, no matter how hard you try using the conscious mind. That's why we discussed how to transform limiting beliefs that act as invisible roadblocks in your efforts to fly high above the limitations of your daily life.

Once you align your conscious and subconscious minds, and begin to trust the insights and new ideas that flow into your mind through your antenna, you become more receptive to the flashes of inspiration, premonitions of danger, etc. it whispers to you, which you can hear only if you are listening attentively through a calm and relaxed mind.

12.3 Function at lower brainwaves

Even when the conscious and subconscious minds broadly agree on a goal, even slight fears, anxieties and doubts in the conscious mind can interfere with the ability of the subconscious mind to project your life to a higher orbit. We have seen an amazing example of this earlier. At the start of the last 200-metre lap

---

117 http://spdrdng.com/posts/conscious-vs-subconscious-processing

in a 600-metre women's race, a runner who didn't have a significant lead over the others suddenly fell flat on her face. She simply got up, ran like the wind, and won the race by beating all the runners who had moved far ahead of her. Where did she suddenly acquire this awesome speed that would have won her the 200-metre world record?

The answer lies in the way our conscious mind works. While running, her conscious mind must have been thinking about all sorts of things such as what happened in earlier races, what pace to maintain, when to increase running speed, joy of winning, fear of losing, etc. All this interferes with the efforts of the subconscious mind to optimise all body processes to achieve maximum running speed. When she fell, the conscious mind must have given up. With her conscious mind empty of thought, the subconscious mind finally had total freedom to unleash the awesome running potential that was always within her. Even more amazing was the fact that after her superhuman effort, she didn't appear to be tired when compared to her competitors who were gasping for breath.

This is how people can do miraculous things spontaneously under life-threatening circumstances that temporarily numb the conscious mind. Such situations shut down the conscious mind and slow the brainwaves down to the theta level normally associated with light sleep. That's why people who have done unbelievable things under life-threatening circumstances often don't remember details of what happened. This also explains how hypnosis can make someone exhibit superhuman strength with their bodies.[118] The unbendable arm that you have experienced enabled you to unleash great physical power while being fully conscious by relaxing your mind at least down to the alpha level.

Once you clearly create a goal, joyously experience it as if already achieved a few times each day using all your senses, and support it with the necessary effort, you can leave the rest to your subconscious mind, without doubting its ability or checking its progress – which would be like uprooting a newly planted sapling every day to check whether roots have started growing!

---

[118] https://www.youtube.com/watch?v=dOtionc_yJE

12.4 Activate your goal-seeking mechanism

You have an automatic goal-seeking mechanism in your brain called the Reticular Activating System. This is like a filter between your conscious mind and your subconscious mind. It takes instructions from your conscious mind and passes them on to your subconscious mind for implementation. It is the gateway to achieving any goal you desire. However, it can't distinguish between 'real' and 'imagined' things, and tends to believe whatever message you give it. Therefore any goal, which you clearly set and imagine using all relevant senses as if already achieved, will be communicated from your conscious to your subconscious mind. The subconscious mind will then bring to your attention all the relevant information that will help you achieve that goal, which it may have filtered out earlier as irrelevant.[119]

This also relates to 'synchronicity' – a concept created by psychiatrist Carl Jung to explain coincidences that don't seem to be as random as we would normally expect.[120] It relates to events that occur with no apparent causal relationship (one doesn't cause the other), yet seem to be meaningfully related in a manner that goes beyond coincidences. For example, unexpectedly meeting someone who can provide you with just the help you need, or finding a published article with exactly the kind of information you have been seeking.

12.5 Use mental contrasting

Mental contrasting creates a strong commitment to achieving a goal by comparing a positive future scenario to its present-day reality. This involves flying with your mind to a future goal after it is reached, and looking back to the current state to see what actions are needed and what obstacles have to be overcome to get there. It helps you to identify gaps in your attributes and resources that hinder the achievement of a desired goal (e.g. becoming a confident public speaker). It has two steps:

1. Imagine achieving a desired future goal and feel its benefits (e.g. speaking confidently in public);

---

119 http://www.make-your-goals-happen.com/reticular-activating-system.html

120 https://en.wikipedia.org/wiki/Synchronicity

2. Mentally identify what prevents you from achieving that future goal, such as obstacles to overcome, resources to find and actions to take (e.g. overcoming your shyness).[121]

In the above example, to become a confident public speaker in the future, you need to develop your self-esteem and self-confidence to overcome your present shyness. A high level of confidence in your ability to overcome your shyness would lead to increased effort and more success, while a low level of confidence would lead to less effort and less success. Attaching a high level of importance to the goal you wish to achieve will thus lead to increased effort and more success, and vice versa.

Mental contrasting helps you to achieve goals that you think are barely within your reach through a determined effort. It will increase your confidence in your ability to reach progressively higher goals by improving your mindset, attitudes, behaviours, knowledge and skills. It will also help you decide which goals are important enough to warrant the effort needed to achieve them. Other factors that will help your efforts to achieve ambitious goals include:

1. Framing your goals clearly with specific time frames (achieve what, how, by when);
2. Stating your goals in terms of promoting positive outcomes instead of preventing negative outcomes (e.g. increasing your self-confidence, instead of overcoming your shyness);
3. Focussing on acquiring new skills (e.g. learning voice projection like stage actors) as opposed to refining your current skills (e.g. practising speaking);
4. Anticipating internal rewards (the joy of achieving a goal) rather than external rewards (awards and recognition).[122]

Mental contrasting will ensure that your personal resources (time, energy, money) are not wasted on goals that you consider unreachable, while maximising your efforts to attain ambitious goals you consider reachable. It also prevents you from reaching a difficult goal after a huge effort, only to realise that it wasn't really worth all that effort. It's like test-driving an

121 https://en.wikipedia.org/wiki/Mental_contrasting

122 http://www.psych.nyu.edu/gollwitzer/OettingenGollwitzer.pdf

expensive car to see if it is worth the large financial commitment needed to own and maintain it.

Mental contrasting can be supported by implementation intentions, which provide a simple mechanism to pre-plan responses to future scenarios that can help or hinder your efforts to achieve goals.

12.6 Use implementation intentions

Mental contrasting enables you to identify present-day obstacles that need to be overcome to achieve a future goal. Implementation intentions, in the form of: *if…, then …* statements enable you to pre-plan your responses to foreseeable future scenarios. It can be used to find best possible responses to potential opportunities as well as obstacles, by drawing on what you learnt from past successes and failures. For example: '*If* I run short of money, *then* I can pawn the gold chain I have.' This is like flying without worrying after pre-planning your responses for typical headwinds, tailwinds, crosswinds and bad weather that characterise your chosen flight path.

This method will create mental links that eliminate the stressful decision-making needed for finding solutions for unexpected problems. It involves identifying possible problems and pre-planning best possible responses that are in line with your goal. You can also use it to condition your mind to overcome any attitudinal or behavioural issues you may have. For example: '*If* I feel angry at someone, *then* I'll take a deep breath to calm my mind before responding.'

Implementation intentions thus provide a simple way to decide on responses to the challenges we may face when trying to reach a goal, by thinking and planning ahead. You can use this technique to discontinue an effort that has become unproductive. For example, when buying a particular stock or commodity that you expected to go up in price, you may decide beforehand: '*If* the price falls 10% below my buying price, *then* I will sell.' This safeguards you from financial losses arising from the belief that the carefully-considered decisions you have made must be good enough to be continued, which may no longer be true in a fast-changing world.

You can use implementation intentions also to identify and seize future opportunities that will help you reach your goal. For example, if you're planning to buy a particular stock or commodity based on recent company and/or market performance, you can decide: '*If* the price falls below 50, *then* I will buy.'

Implementation intentions can also help you to get started towards achieving a goal. Having implementation intentions that relate to when, where and how you will get started, can make you three times more likely to succeed than by doing only mental contrasting (Oettingen & Gollwitzer, 2010).

12.7 Use mental contrasting with implementation intentions

This provides a powerful combination that greatly increases your ability to achieve challenging goals. Mental contrasting provides a strong motivation to achieve a challenging goal by letting you mentally experience the future benefits when compared with the present-day realities. Implementation intentions free your mind from the distraction of searching for ways to overcome foreseeable obstacles or seize foreseeable opportunities. It leads to a swift, stress-free and near-automatic allocation of mental energy when such obstacles or opportunities are encountered, without worrying about when and how to respond.

Mental contrasting for goal-selection followed by *if… then …* preplanning, thus enables you to overcome obstacles and seize opportunities on your way to achieving your goals. This simple combination prevents your efforts to achieve ambitious goals from getting derailed by obstacles that you will invariably face. It also provides a way to manage negative indications about your progress towards a desired goal, so you can decide either to drop the goal or change your approach for achieving it.

This combination also provides a very effective way of eliminating procrastination (delaying something you should be doing because you don't really want to do it) and indecisiveness (inability to make decisions). These arise either from having to do something which appears boring or unpleasant, or not knowing when and what to do next. Say for example that your good intentions to develop your Health dimension often get forgotten. Implementation intentions such as, '*If* I feel hungry, *then* I will eat a banana instead of a candy bar' will overcome any initial reluctance to adopting healthy eating habits and also tell you what to do in a typical situation.

Combining mental contrasting with implementation intentions will enable you to change your lifestyle and habits for developing all six dimensions of success for flying higher than you ever imagined possible. To achieve ambitious goals by overcoming setbacks, you need to be a realistic optimist as opposed to an unrealistic optimist.

12.8 Use realistic optimism

To be able to achieve ambitious goals (BHAGs), you need to understand the vital difference between believing you will succeed, and believing you will succeed easily. This is the difference between being a realistic optimist and an unrealistic optimist.

Realistic optimists believe they will succeed, but that success requires effort, careful planning, persistence, and choosing the right goals (using mental contrasting). They recognise the need for giving serious thought to how they will deal with obstacles (through implementation intentions). Unrealistic optimists, on the other hand, believe that the universe will reward them for all their positive thinking, with little or no effort on their part.

Studies have shown that people who believe they can achieve a goal (optimists), as opposed to those who doubt it (pessimists), have a higher level of success in achieving it. However, those who believe they will succeed easily (unrealistic optimists) have a lower level of success than those who believe they need to work to achieve success through persistent effort (realistic optimists).[123]

So it's important to believe you will succeed despite setbacks (using your 'YES' power), instead of believing success will come to you effortlessly. Expecting the journey to be difficult makes you prepared for the challenges ahead using implementation intentions. This preparation will increase your confidence in your own ability to achieve ambitious goals despite any setbacks.

12.9 Use your imagination

Creating something with your mind using all your senses is one of the keys to achieving a material goal in your life. More than 10,000 years ago, cavemen in the region that is now France used visualisation to help them on their hunts. They painted pictures of the animals they hunted on the walls of their caves, to make every hunter focus on hunting them. By the light of the tribe's fire, the images seemed to be actually moving. These images became so real in their minds that some of them actually threw spears at the drawings! The marks are still there to this day.[124]

[123] https://hbr.org/2011/05/be-an-optimist-without-being-a/

[124] http://tinyurl.com/metaartsandsciences-org

In his pioneering book, 'Think and grow rich', Napoleon Hill said that we can achieve any realistic goal if we continue thinking of that goal. However, if we keep thinking that we can't achieve a goal, our subconscious will try to make sure that we won't achieve it.[125] For example, say you have to give a speech, and you are dissatisfied about its content and feel nervous about your delivery. The more nervous you feel, the greater the chance your speech will be a disaster. On the other hand, rather than worrying about your speech, you can use your 'YES' power and playfully imagine that your speech contains fascinating information, and the feel joy of hearing a rapturous applause at the end of it. This will replace your feeling of anxiety with the excitement of delivering a memorable speech, and enable your subconscious mind to attract the new ideas you seek.

12.10 Use different thinking skills

Just the way you would select a different gear in a car to suit the road condition, different situations require different thinking:

- Intuitive thinking (sensing instead of reasoning)
- Focused thinking (clarifying the essence of things)
- Creative thinking (exploring new ideas – divergent thinking)
- Strategic thinking (selecting the optimum choice – convergent thinking)

1. Use intuitive thinking to 'download' new ideas. First do your 'homework' by studying all relevant information. Then relax your mind and do something totally unrelated to let your subconscious mind work on it without interference. The subconscious mind will process the information and come up new insights and ideas that logical thinking alone won't provide. This often happens at unexpected moments, if you are 'listening'.
2. Use focused thinking to clarify the purpose. Without focused thinking we may be solving the wrong problem. Mental contrasting will help you to do this. The idea is to find a simple and elegant solution instead of an irrelevant or unnecessarily complicated one. For example, as the

[125] http://eventualmillionaire.com/Resources/ThinkandGrowRich.pdf

popular story goes, using a suitably modified pencil in space instead of an expensive pen that could put ink to paper without depending on gravity.[126]

3. Use creative thinking to explore new options. Free the mind from its information-processing limitations. Suspend judgement and go beyond conventional logic. Provoke the mind to focus on 'crazy' ideas and explore out-of-the-box concepts, non-judgementally. You will end up with a whole series of options of diverse viability.
4. Use strategic thinking to select the optimum solution. Examine each identified option for viability. Evaluate each option under best and worst case scenarios. Select the best option with the highest probability of success under foreseeable conditions.

12.11 Focus on behaviour instead of goals

Our emotions cause us to behave in certain ways: feeling happy makes us smile, worrying makes us frown, etc. The reverse is also true: a forced smile makes us feel happy, a forced frown makes us feel worried, etc. Several studies show that firming your muscles (e.g. a clenched fist or teeth) can help strengthen your willpower that will boost your ability to withstand immediate pain, overcome tempting food, consume unpleasant medicines, act on disturbing information, etc. provided you see the long-term benefits of doing so. Your bodies can thus help strengthen your willpower and assist you with the self-correction needed for attaining goals.[127] For example, by making a clenched fist to resist the temptation to buy sugary snacks in a cafeteria, you are far more likely to buy healthy food.

Visualisation is not enough to achieve a goal. This is because people who believe in visualisation and positive thinking typically focus on the goal instead of the behaviour that will lead to its achievement. Self-help books and gurus have been saying for years that thinking like a millionaire will magically make you grow rich. Such unrealistic optimism rarely produces the desired result, mainly because of not putting in the effort needed to achieve such an ambitious goal, not being prepared to overcome setbacks, etc. Gautama

126 http://www.scientificamerican.com/article/fact-or-fiction-nasa-spen/

127 http://papers.ssrn.com/sol3/papers.cfm?abstract_id=1790324

Buddha clarified his declaration: *All that we are is the result of what we have thought,* with his last words: *Work hard to gain your own salvation.*[128] He thus summarised the importance of integrating positive thoughts with focussed effort.

12.12 Use power-posing

By acting as if you are a certain type of person, you become that person. You can use this principle to achieve your goals. For example, we express power through open, expansive postures, while we express powerlessness through closed, contractive postures. A study showed that high-power posers experienced increased feelings of power and tolerance for risk even after one minute, while low-power posers exhibited the opposite pattern. Power-posing can produce positive psychological, physiological, and behavioural changes.[129]

These extend beyond mere thinking and feeling, to physiological and subsequent behavioural choices that will lead to the achievement of your goals. Power poses that make you feel powerful include taking up more space while sitting or standing, standing tall with legs spread wide, breathing deep, hands on hips, etc. This is similar to what you did earlier to make your arm unbendable. Just one minute of dominant power-posing can make you become more powerful, irrespective of your age or current physical state.

Adopting the physical gait and posture of a young person triggers an immediate response in the body of a person of any age. Just acting young can positively influence physical capacities such as strength, memory, mood, better eyesight and hearing. We can 'trick' the body into being at its best in exactly the same way that conventional thinking about getting older 'trick' us into believing we 'just can't do that anymore'.[130]

---

[128] http://www.buddhanet.net/e-learning/buddhism/lifebuddha/2_31lbud.htm

[129] http://pss.sagepub.com/content/21/10/1363

[130] http://staying-ageless.com/?p=2414

12.13 Helpful suggestions

Here are some techniques that will help your efforts to overcome obstacles and achieve your goals. They are adaptations of some exercises suggested by Richard Wiseman and validated by research studies:[131]

1. *Unhappiness*: Smile as wide as possible and hold your forced smile for about 20 seconds to make you really feel happy and give you the courage to continue. Such synthetic happiness feels as good as real happiness.
2. *Lethargy*: Make a fist, or contract your biceps, or press your thumb and first finger together, or grip something in your hand, or use your YES power to increase your determination and willpower.
3. *Depression*: Regular exercise acts as a natural anti-depressant by releasing chemicals and hormones that trigger feelings of wellbeing while improving learning and memory.
4. *Overworking*: If you have to put in a lot of intellectual effort in your studies or work, adopt a work-rest cycle with about 90 minutes of effort followed by a 15-minute break.
5. *Lack of confidence*: Power-posing with deep breathing will immediately increase your self-esteem and self-confidence.
6. *Learning difficulties*: Do regular exercise especially prior to learning, take breaks between study times, learn your material in related chunks, and play computer games that involve problem solving.
7. *Procrastination*: Slightly clench your teeth, tense your muscles, breathe deep and start doing the first part of whatever it is you are avoiding. Things get easier once you start, just like how pushing a car becomes easier once you get it moving.
8. *Indecisiveness:* Using your YES power will make any wrong decision a learning opportunity. As Dire Straits sang in Once Upon a Time in The West: *Sitting on a fence that's a dangerous course. You could even catch a bullet from the peace-keeping force.*
9. *Lack of perseverance*: Breathe deep, clench your teeth, sit up straight and cross your arms when the going gets tough to increase your perseverance.

---

131 http://www.theguardian.com/science/2012/jun/30/self-help-positive-thinking

10. *Negotiation*: Use soft chairs, since they are mentally associated with soft behaviour, which will help negotiations by reducing mental resistance.
11. *Persuasion*: To attract people to your way of thinking, nod your head subtly while listening, match their physical postures and speech patterns, and feel loving kindness towards them.
12. *Overeating*: Chew each mouthful at least 32 times and eat with your non-dominant hand to prevent mindlessly overeating.
13. *Junk food addiction*: Resist temptation by thinking of the resulting health hazards while power-posing, making a fist, contracting your muscles and breathing deeply.
14. *Smoking*: Use the same technique, or smoke with total mindfulness to feel how smoking really affects your energy despite any initial boost.

12.14 See setbacks as gifts

This is about flying after falling. In your attempts to fly high you will invariably encounter serious setbacks (the higher you fly, the further you could fall). Your emotional immune system will make sure that any disappointment will not last long, especially if a burning ambition drives you forward.

You can use the techniques you have discovered so far to generate positive energy and create a learning experience from any setback on your way to achieving your goals. Say you had an accident with your car (similar to the crashes you may experience until you master the art of flying). A typical reaction would be to feel bad about what happened. You can transform this negative emotion instantly by changing your point of view and using 'YES' power. Try saying to others with great enthusiasm: *Hey, guess what happened today. I crashed my car ('YES'). Now I can get all the little problems also fixed!*

Simply by changing your point of view, adopting an empowering body posture, breathing deeply, and unleashing your 'YES' power you can deal with any situation no matter how threatening it seems. Most importantly, you will generate more mental and physical energy when most needed to deal with any challenging situation.

Many bright students fail their exams not due to a lack of knowledge, but due to a fear of loss of face associated with failing. Going to the exam fully energised and thinking that you will either be the best-in-class or the worst-in-class ('YES') will make you feel good and clear your mind of stress and anxiety.

In this relaxed state of mind, you will easily recall all what you have learnt. However, if despite your best efforts, you fail the exam, accept the result with 'YES' power and see what new doors the universe is opening for you, since passing an exam is no guarantee of success in life.

What happens to us, or what people say or do to us, is rarely under our control. But, how we perceive it and respond to it is totally under our control. 'YES' power creates a win-win situation, no matter what happens. Good if we win; good if we 'lose' because we can eliminate 'weak shots' in our game of life to achieve the highest levels of success. 'YES' power thus creates a new holistic paradigm for understanding life, beyond the dualistic interpretation of events as good or bad, winning or losing, etc.

Part Five:

Your Flight Training Schedule

13. Your training schedule

What we found we threw away;
What we couldn't find we kept

As we grow older, we acquire negative thoughts and habits that gradually hide our vast inborn human potential. To excel at mental flying, you need to find and throw away the mental limitations and roadblocks that you have accumulated over the years.

The Buddha taught that: *You are your own refuge and you are your own saviour.* He urged people to help themselves since everyone has the ability to do so. You can't rely on other beings or things because we and everything in the world is impermanent, and therefore not dependable. This means you have to take total responsibility for your own life, without leaving it to others.[132]

13.1 Daily task schedule

This is your daily training schedule that will develop all six dimensions of success. At the end of each day, tick what you have done. Aim for a small improvement every day and celebrate each little success you achieve. Doing each task for 21 days will help you to integrate it into your daily routine, which will make it an almost unconscious habit thereafter.

You probably will not have time to do all tasks every day. You can spread them over a convenient period, except for the five Tibetan rites; each of these has to be done preferably at the same time each day on an empty stomach;

[132] http://www.buddhapadipa.org/dhamma-corner/seek-your-own-refuge/

you can begin with 1-5 repetitions of each exercise and gradually increase up to 21 times.

All the practical techniques explained in this book are summarised below. The second column shows the relevant section in the book. After repeating each task at least 21 times, you will begin to develop the five qualities of a self-motivated highflyer:

1. Self-awareness
2. Self-confidence
3. Self-assessment
4. Self-improvement
5. Self-discipline.

			1	2	3	4	5	6	7	8	9	10	11	12	13	14	15	16	17	18	19	20	21
Developing my Heart																							
1.	8.1b1&2	Loved & forgave myself																					
2.	8.1b3	Forgave others who have hurt me																					
3.	8.1b4	Felt grateful for everything in my life																					
4.	8.1b5	Blessed others nonverbally																					
5.	8.1b6	Practised the 100-0 rule																					
Developing my Mind																							
6.	3.2	Used a chance to switch from 'being-good' to 'getting-better'																					
7.	6.4	Transformed my negative emotions & thoughts																					
8.	6.8	Identified & overwrote my limiting beliefs																					
9.	8.2b	Did a mental exercise																					
10.	8.2d3	Drank enough water																					
11.	8.2d4	Did the 20+20+10+10sec exercise to relax & energise my brain																					
12.	8.2e4	Used my non-dominant hand to balance my brain																					
13.	8.2e6	Did image streaming to balance my brain																					
14.	8.2e8	Did 'super brain yoga' to balance my brain																					
15.	8.2k	Emptied my mind with relaxed breathing																					
16.	8.2m5	Read out a book or newspaper loud to boost memory power																					
17.	8.2n	Used memory pegs to remember things without writing down																					

			1	2	3	4	5	6	7	8	9	10	11	12	13	14	15	16	17	18	19	20	21
18.	8.2o	Used mental correlations to remember names																					
19.	12.7	Used mental contrasting with implementation intentions																					
20.	12.8	Used realistic optimism																					
Developing my Passion																							
21.	4.5	Used power-posing to energise my mind & body																					
22.	4.6	Switched from 'NO' energy to 'YES' power																					
23.	8.3a2	Rubbed my ears vigorously with palms to energise my body																					
24.	8.3a3	Did 10 abdominal power breaths with blowing out stale air																					
25.	8.3a4	Did 30 body squats with synchronised breathing & relaxed 30secs																					
26.	8.3b1	Did something I really love																					
27.	8.3b2	Showed my passion with no inhibitions																					
28.	8.3b3	Associated with passionate people																					
Developing my Focus																							
29.	8.4a2	Circled each hand to the side, over the head and vertically down																					
30.	8.4a3	Captured & held a visual image in my mind																					
31.	8.4a4	Counted & chewed each mouthful at least 32 times																					
32.	8.4a5	Practised the 'unbendable arm'																					

Developing my Body																							
33.	8.5b	Did Master Del Pe's 8 exercises to develop my energy centres																					
34.	8.5c	Did the Chi Kung energy exercise																					
35.	8.5d	Did the 5 Tibetan rites for rejuvenation																					
Developing my Health																							
36.	8.211	De-stressed through conscious deep breathing																					
37.	8.212	De-stressed by shaking the body																					
38.	8.214	De-stressed by stretching both arms up while leaning back																					
39.	8.215	De-stressed by chanting 'Om' to relax & activate energy centres																					
40.	8.216	De-stressed by having a backup plan																					
41.	8.217	De-stressed by saying 'no' firmly but caringly																					
42.	8.6k1	Drank water with fresh lime/lemon juice on an empty stomach																					
43.	8.6k2	Drank several cups of leaf green tea																					
44.	8.6k3	Avoided all forms of processed food & beverages																					
45.	8.6k4	Ate & drank 75% of alkaline foods (fresh fruits, raw vegetables)																					
46.	8.6k5	Chewed each mouthful until liquid by counting at least 32 times																					
47.	8.6k6	Ate a lot of greens (ideally raw) to oxygenate the cells																					
48.	8.6k8	Did some physical activity (walking, sports, dancing...)																					
49.	8.6m	Practised healing codes (6-minute antidote to stress)																					
50.	8.6n	Practised Tapping (Emotional Freedom Technique – EFT)																					

Welcome to the growing community of higher flyers
who are discovering the 'treasure of treasures' hidden within them
and leading others to a higher level of human consciousness.

References

Bach, R. D. (1970). *Jonathan Livingston Seagull.* New York: Avon Books.

Bandler, R. (2008). *Get the life you want: The secrets to quick and lasting life change with neuro-linguistic programming.* Deerfield Beach, Florida: Health Communications.

Biehl, B. (1989). *Increasing your leadership confidence: Fine-tune your leadership skills.* Sisters: Questar Publishers.

Capra, F. (1983). *The Tao of physics: An exploration of the parallels between modern physics and Eastern mysticism.* London: Fontana Paperbacks.

Castaneda, C. (1998). *The teachings of Don Juan: A Yaqui way of knowledge.* New York: Washington Square Press.

Cherry, K. A. (2008). The Milgram obedience experiment. Retrieved from http://psychology.about.com/od/socialinfluence/fl/What-Is-Obedience.htm

Chuen, L. K. (1991). *The way of energy: mastering the Chinese art of internal strength with chi kung exercise.* New York: Simon & Schuster Inc.

Covey, S. R. (2004). *The 8th habit: From effectiveness to greatness.* New York: Free Press.

Davis, A. (1970). *Let's eat right to keep fit.* New York: Signet.

Davis, A. (1972). *Let's get well.* New York: Signet.

Dean, D. & Mihalasky, J. (1974). *Executive ESP.* New Jersey: Prentice-Hall.

Del Pe, M. (2006). *From success to fulfilment: Applying the wisdom of the Himalayan masters.* Bhopal, India: Manjul Books.

Erdmann, E., & Stover, D. (1991). *Beyond a world divided: Human values in the brain-mind science of Roger Sperry.* Nebraska: Authors Choice Press.

Ferris, T. (2007). *The 4-hour workweek: Escape 9-5, live anywhere, and join the new rich.* New York: Crown Publishers.

Fuhrman, J. (2011). *Super immunity: The essential nutrition guide for boosting your body's defenses to live longer, stronger and disease free.* New York: Harper Collins Publishers.

Gallwey, W. T. (1974). *The inner game of tennis.* New York: Random House.

Gardner, H. E. (2006). *Multiple intelligences: New horizons in theory and practice.* New York: Basic Books.

Gilbert, D. T., Pinel, E. C., Wilson, T. D., Blumberg, S. J., & Wheatley, T. (1998). *Immune neglect: A source of durability bias in affective forecasting.* Journal of Personality and Social Psychology, 75, 617-638.

Gladwell M. (2005). *Blink: The power of thinking without thinking.* London: Penguin Books.

Gladwell, M. (2008). *Outliers: The story of success.* New York: Little, Brown and Company.

Goleman, D. (1995). *Emotional intelligence: Why it can matter more than IQ.* New York: Bantam Books.

Heider J. (1986). The Tao of Leadership. Aldershot, Hants, England: Wild House.

Hill, N. (1960). *Think and grow rich.* New York: Fawcett Books.

Jinadasa, A. N. (2015). An empirical five-dimensional holistic model of leadership. In A.N.M.Wahid & C.R.Amaro (Eds.) *Proceedings of the Australasian conference on business and social sciences 2015, Sydney,* pp. 316-330.

Kahneman D. (2011). *Thinking, fast and slow.* London: Penguin Books.

Kendrick, M. (2007). *The great cholesterol con: The truth about what really causes heart disease and how to avoid it.* London: John Blake Publishing.

Loyd, A., & Johnson, B. (2010). *The healing code.* Peoria: Intermedia Publishing Group.

Narada Thera, (1987). *The Buddha and his Teachings.* Colombo, Sri Lanka: The Lever Brothers Cultural Conservation Trust.

Oettingen, G., & Gollwitzer, P. M. (2010). Strategies of setting and implementing goals. In J.E.Maddux & J.P.Tangney (Eds.) *Social psychological foundations of clinical psychology.* New York: The Guilford Press.

Pauling, L. (1986). *How to live longer and feel better.* New York: W.H.Freeman.

Pearce, J. C. (2004). *The biology of transcendence: A blueprint of the human spirit.* Rochester, Vermont: Park Street Press.

Pickert, K. (2014). The mindful revolution. *Time, 183*(4), 34-38.

Robinson, K., & Aronica, L. (2009). *The element: How changing your passion changes everything.* New York: Penguin Group.

Trungpa, C. (2011). *The path is the goal: A basic handbook of Buddhist meditation.* Boston, Massachusetts: Shambhala Publications.

Watson, J. B. (1930). *Behaviorism.* New Brunswick, New Jersey: Transaction Publishers.

Wigmore, A. (1983). *The Hippocrates diet and health program.* Pennington: Avery Publishing.

Printed in the United States
By Bookmasters